PRIMARY
POLITICS

Charles Brereton

Peter E. Randall Publisher
Portsmouth, New Hampshire
2003

Peter E. Randall Publisher
Box 4726
Portsmouth, NH 03802
603-431-5667
www.perpublisher.com
Fax: 603-431-3566

ISBN 1-931807-17-5
Library of Congress Control Number: 2003096205

Cover photograph: Voting in the New Hampshire presidential
primary on Town Meeting Day, March 11, 1952. From the
National Archives.

Back cover photograph: President Dwight Eisenhower visiting
Concord on June 23, 1955. Dwight D. Eisenhower Library.

To five special friends in the fair city of Portsmouth:
Tess Denney, her daughter, Sume, Sume's children, Aidan and Ella
Rosemary, and their father, Sean Caughran

December 26, 2003

To Sandy Hoch,
Thank you for helping to
save our Republic in '68 —
Love.

ALSO BY CHARLES BRERETON

First Step to the White House (1979)

New Hampshire Notables (1986)

First in the Nation (1987)

First Primary (1987)

CONTENTS

INTRODUCTION

> But that's a good word—primary. That's how this state thinks of
> itself anyway. Primary all the way!
>> —Ferris, the lead character in *The Wisest Man in America*,
>> by W. D. Wetherell

J UST PRIOR TO HIS ARRIVAL AT THE CAMP of Prince Faisal in the movie *Lawrence of Arabia*, T. E. Lawrence (played by Peter O'Toole) was asked by Colonel Brighton, "What are you to do for the Arab Bureau?" Lawrence responded, "I'm to appreciate the situation."

The same expression should be applied to every reporter who visits the premier primary state each quadrennium. Some reporters who have been honing their craft and have covered the lead-off primary with distinction always seem able to accomplish this task.

The same can't be said of many others who repeatedly make this trek to what has been referred to as the Switzerland of America.

It is not an exaggeration to say that in virtually every presidential election year, reporters often leave here shaking their heads in bewilderment about what has taken place. And instead of filing reports that provide a sense of the history and context of what has occurred, time and again they will confess that they are clueless about not only what has transpired, but why.

This is one primary state where shoe leather still counts for something. It is not a myth that candidates must make contact with as many voters as they possibly can; it happens to be at the top of just about every campaign manager's "to do" list for his or her candidate.

However, this is not a place where the hopeful who manages

to shake the most hands always wins, for there are several other factors at play. It is a rare primary in which the aspirant with the highest number of days visiting this state of over 1.2 million residents also wins the Republican or Democratic primary.

Any serious candidate must also build an organization, raise sufficient funds, prepare and deliver a media blitz and, most important of all, sharpen a message that in the final week enables that hopeful to separate himself or herself from the remainder of the pack.

All of this is accomplished on a terrain that is vastly different from a mega- or even a medium-sized state. It is just about impossible (especially for a Democrat) to expect a major officeholder to carry the day for a candidate. He or she has to earn it, not have it handed to him or her, as then Texas governor George W. Bush found out the hard way in the last primary.

The Granite State is in no way similar to a place like Illinois— where usually the Democratic presidential primary is a primary of one: If you have the mayor of Chicago in your corner, you also have the Illinois primary in your pocket.

There seems to be an endless debate concerning the first primary state. Is it or is it not a North American version of a Yanomami tribe of Brazil, a true Neolithic group that had lived in nearly absolute isolation until recently? Not a few reporters seem to carry that image of this state's residents in their minds, particularly concerning those living in the sparsely populated, beautiful and remote North Country.

Then there is another preconception—that the voters of this state simply don't know what to think about the race for the White House until the voters in the Iowa caucuses tell them who is presidential timber and who is not.

That just is not the case and things certainly didn't pan out that way in 2000; Arizona senator John McCain ignored the first caucus and, without any sort of "bounce" out of the Midwest, somehow managed to defeat George Bush by a landslide here.

Time and again this small state has to act as a brake on the national media's playing the role of kingmaker and guarantee that the race for the nomination of our two national parties isn't proclaimed over after just a single Midwestern and a northern New England state have been heard from.

Although the media's persistent desire to engage in incestuous amplification seems to increase with every presidential election, there is always the hope that they will somehow comprehend the fact that Iowa merely sets the table; it is up to New Hampshire to determine the seating arrangements so that the dinner party is not proclaimed over just as the appetizer has been served.

There have been 13 primaries since 1952, when the names of presidential contenders were first placed on the ballots alongside those of delegates (which had been listed beginning in 1916). Surely this is long enough to discern the patterns and trends that help determine why the voters act the way they do. It is up to the reader of this work to decide whether I have succeeded in deciphering what some of these patterns and trends have been.

The primary is certainly not the final word in the race for the nominations of our two major political parties. Almost without exception the choices in the contests are winnowed down, but not closed down completely. Anyone proposing any sort of change in the system has to make a case that the change does not stifle the opportunity for candidates other than frontrunners or the wealthy self-funded to be heard.

It is unfortunate that the national party leaders have failed to mitigate the process of frontloading, where more and more states hold primaries in February and March instead of in March, April, May and early June as in yesteryear.

The solution to this problem is a simple one: more caucuses— so many more that there are equal numbers of primaries and caucuses instead of the 40 primaries held in 2000.

One of the more troubling issues, as the race for '04 unfolds, is that although there is little support for a national primary, this nation is moving closer to one with every passing quadrennium.

It isn't a one-day national primary that this nation is moving toward, thankfully, but a one-month one; this means that, in a nation of this massive size in both population and geography, there is so much ground to cover that the calendar becomes increasingly compressed and money (and hence TV ads) become the coin of the realm.

Although national party leaders have done little to reverse the trend of frontloading, at least in some states legislators are realizing that since voters won't take the time to vote in sometimes meaningless primaries, the public should be spared large campaign and election expenditures.

If an equal number of primaries and caucuses can be established, an important step will be taken to build a national playing field that is as level as possible for serious candidates for the Oval Office.

Money (and thus advertising) will still matter, but so, too, will the years of base-building in states, along with the courting of significant constituencies. This will help guarantee that we will still have a chance to elect someone to our highest office who understands what lives are like for so many citizens of this land.

That contact with lower officeholders, activists and citizens helps keep our presidents grounded; after all, it is an office that tends to isolate those elected to serve there.

And a system that forces candidates (most of whom hold office inside the Beltway) to travel to places like Berlin, Laconia and Claremont, New Hampshire, is something our political process should embrace.

With yet another primary fast approaching, once again the call is heard in newspaper editorials and columns about the need for change, given how "unrepresentative" the first primary state is. But before this nation concocts a series of regional primaries, one hopes it will ask the question: Will this in fact actually improve the nomination process?

The first state to try to poach on our solitary first-in-the-nation primary status was Florida in 1972. Given the fact that the Sunshine State has yet to achieve some degree of consistency in being able to simply count their votes, would the nomination process achieve a state of bliss if Florida were to replace the Granite State at the head of the primary parade?

With every presidential election, our country is moving closer to a de facto national primary—now to extend over about a month. This time frame does little to help lesser-known hopefuls convert strong showings in Iowa and/or New Hampshire into campaigns that then achieve the Republican or Democratic nomination.

Yet in the event of a failure of one or two hopefuls to begin to break free of the rest of the pack in that first month, isn't this calendar heading down that road called the law of unexpected consequences? By eliminating the march from January to June and having instead a bottleneck of mostly primaries in February and March, could not this avalanche of voting bury the crowded field of candidates instead of elevating just one or two to the front of the pack (which has taken place so often in the past)?

Such a logjam after just a month of voting could well leave several months of a "dead zone" as the leading contenders are left to scavenge for support in just a few remaining primaries and caucuses.

If such a logjam were to occur it would mean several months of very little meaningful primary and caucus activity, thus leaving the public even more disengaged than in the past. But there could be a silver lining if such a scenario does actually pan out: For the first time in more than half a century we might actually have a national party convention with more than a single ballot.

Time and time again this state has proven to be a rather slippery slope for frontrunners, as George W. Bush of Texas found out in the year 2000. One of the more interesting aspects of this first direct vote is how little it has changed since the names of candidates were first placed on the ballots in 1952 and another frontrunner, President Harry Truman, also managed to slip on the icy terrain.

This says something about the Granite State: This lack of change provides a consistency in how the primaries are conducted, and the complete absence of any favorite sons (or daughters) from every ballot guarantees a level playing field for all.

One of the perpetual struggles in our democratic system is the contest of wills between those who rule and those who are ruled. We are a long way from "King Caucus," when just the members of the House and Senate in the nation's capital decided who the nominees of the major parties for president would be.

However, there is still a contest between those in the national political (as well as business) elite who, without taking a formal vote, manage to let the nation know whom they generally support, and the determination of those who begin to arrive in force in the caucuses and primaries that soon give shape and cohesion to what often becomes the antiestablishment selection.

Frequently the voters in the first primary are caught between the proverbial rock and a hard place. If they decide to merely ratify the anointed choice of the elite they are in the good graces of the powerful—but at what cost to a spirited and competitive electoral process?

It just happens that this is a cost the voters here are willing to meet about every quadrennium; instead of shutting down the nomination contest, the media is told: Not so fast—this contest should not be declared over after just Iowa and New Hampshire have been heard from.

First primary voters always seem to try to send several messages with their ballots, and one they always have been able to deliver to the media is "you report, we decide."

So their lot is cast with a Kefauver rather than a Truman, a Hart rather than a Mondale, a McCain over yet another Bush. They vote not necessarily for the person they believe will be the next president of the United States, but make sure the primaries soon to follow in so many other states retain some relevance.

The state with the first direct vote also provides a sense of place in a nation that many would agree offers far too much change in far too many locations.

The southern tier of the Granite State has been one of the fastest growing regions in the Northeast for decades. However, there are still many towns (especially in the North Country) that cling with tenacity to small-town traditions such as town meetings and local control and responsibility—which all help to provide a sense of rootedness (and separateness) that has been forsaken in far too many other places.

Such a setting permits the voters to judge for themselves and without the power brokers, filters and interpreters seen so often elsewhere. Every primary is a search for a candidate who seems to be more grounded than the others and also able to offer a succinct and reasoned argument as to why this individual should be our maximum national leader. And it doesn't hurt that the candidate or two who finally emerges from the pack in the final weeks is able to offer ideas and proposals that are more than words on a position paper or given in a speech, but are backed up by real-world experience that has helped shape and test such ideas and programs.

The voters always seem to be in search of a candidate who provides this strong feeling of being grounded—an individual who is comfortable within his own skin and what he believes in, rather than someone trying his best to recall what his consultants and pollsters have programmed him to deliver as the message of the day.

It also helps that the primary is a venue that has been around for some time, for many voters have a chance not only to listen to most if not all the major contenders, but also to reach back in memory and compare and contrast the current crop of hopefuls with those who have preceded them in primaries past. These are reference points that simply can't be found in other states.

Having political leaders and the news media returning to the same venue every leap year might strike some as being unfair, but it provides an opportunity that just can't be equaled elsewhere—and certainly couldn't be had if the system were altered to a national or even a series of regional primaries.

There are those opposed to this state's historic role who often argue that because the state's population is so small, it would be a fairer process if a much larger state were first instead. Yet such a change would deprive the lesser known hopefuls of an opportunity to be heard. In other words, the way to guarantee the complete mediaization of our nominating campaigns would be to replace New Hampshire with California. Is there anyone willing to make the case that such a change would lead us to a stronger democracy as well as to an enhanced nomination system?

Even those with a superficial understanding of the way we nominate the presidential candidates would have to concede that such a change would not improve what is in place—albeit ad hoc—today.

After the November '04 vote is tabulated (and who knows—maybe the candidate with the most votes will actually become our president), there will be yet another effort to study the nomination process—at least by the Democrats.

This is understandable because the Grand Old Party has always let the other party take the lead in this domain, and it is also understandable given the fact that the GOP has won eight of the 13 presidential elections since 1952.

The GOP obviously has less motivation to "reform" the system and it seems rather comfortable in the organizational role model it has found—the corporate structure. Therefore, it is quite unusual

for the party of Lincoln and Theodore Roosevelt to suffer the kind
of donnybrook Democrats find themselves having so often. (It's
not a stretch to say the organizational role model the Democrats
have managed to latch onto is that of a dysfunctional family.)

The party that resolves its nomination fight the earliest usually
wins the presidency. But if the Democrats lead the charge for a substantial revision in the primary process, will this by itself shorten
the odds for this party to win back the Oval Office?

Since the Democrats have lost more presidential elections than
they've won since 1952 there might be a temptation to blame the
existing process for this fact. But that process is essentially the
same for both parties and it might behoove national Democratic
leaders to look more at whom they've nominated rather than how
they were nominated.

To this observer of more than three decades of primaries, the
way these campaigns are covered often leaves something to be
desired. A surface understanding of this state seems to be par for
the course for far too many reporters. And you can be certain that
in '04, if a candidate does take a dive into a mosh pit or falls off the
stage at the quadrennial pancake flipping contest in Manchester, it
will garner far more television exposure than any policy address a
candidate happens to deliver.

No doubt once again there will be little sense of the history of
what the primary has meant to this nation since 1952. But despite
this and other limitations, one or two candidates always seem to
come to the forefront and the voters always seem to grasp what
type of leader our nation is seeking.

By doing this time and time again the first primary state in the
end permits every voter to "appreciate the situation."

I

THE RODNEY DANGERFIELD
OF PRESIDENTIAL PRIMARIES

New Hampshire's distinctiveness started early. In a country that
prides itself on its feistiness and freedom from outside direction, it
has always been even feistier and less fettered by authority. Before
the Revolutionary War, New Hampshire was almost an outlaw
colony, its great fortunes made by poachers in the king's forests
and smugglers avoiding taxes. It was the first colony with an independent government and was fighting the British before the
Minutemen stood at Lexington and Concord.
                              —*The Almanac of American Politics 2002*

MUCH HAS BEEN WRITTEN about New Hampshire's first-in-the-
nation presidential primary and not all of it complimentary.
New Hampshire has been referred to as "another tiny, atypical
state," "that marginal state," "one of the three or four most unrepresentative states," and its primary as "a farce," "the state's private
practical joke on the rest of the country," "a quadrennial coldwater
fiesta to hook the tourist dollar," "that deep frozen inconclusive,
misleading carnival of political egotism and pop ideology," and
"New England's oldest winter carnival."

In addition, the primary is considered to be "widely unrepresentative of the nation," "an exercise in perversity," and even Art
Buchwald has proclaimed it to be a "cold and Loeb-infected land."

Since this is just a small sample of some of the negative com-
mentary directed at the Granite State, it is obviously a strong con-

tender for the award for being the Rodney Dangerfield of presidential primaries.

Critics of the premier primary have found an inviting target. They often perceive this state as a Lilliputian and frozen location that shouldn't have such an inordinate amount of power to determine who the next president of the United States will be.

However, there are those who defend the initial primary. One is David Hoeh, author in 1994 of *1968 • McCarthy • New Hampshire*, who wrote,

> The final acknowledgment is to the genius of those who put the New Hampshire presidential primary into the political landscape of this nation. The New Hampshire presidential primary is a modest door to the political system which opens by time lock every four years. It offers a neutral process, available to any one to use, but is clearly one of those safety valves in the political system which allows the energy of change to be expressed, tested, proven, or released with little or no threat to the entire construction of the republic.

Despite all the criticism leveled at the state holding the primary it does have its compensation. According to a report by the Library and Archives of New Hampshire's Political Tradition issued in August 2000, "The one-year economic impact of the 2000 primary, including $33 million in publicity benefits, was $264 million. That's a fraction of the state's overall economy, about six-tenths of 1 percent of the state's $42 billion gross state product."

The state legislature revised the law in 1949 to permit a complete primary: The names of candidates would be included on the ballot with delegate hopefuls; only the latter had been included from 1916 until the revision. It didn't take long for the primary to be discovered.

The Jan. 14, 1952 issue of *Newsweek* featured a cover with Lebanon farmer Alec K. Pringle on a day that the temperature dipped as low as 20 degrees below zero. The three-page article on the first primary ended with a page of a dozen photos including this caption: Lebanon resident Alec Pringle shown tending one of his cows on his farm, stating, "Taft is the best man. I wouldn't greatly favor a military man and I think that Taft can win."

Since the appearance of farmer Pringle there have been 20 covers from *Time* and *Newsweek* published about some of the candidates who've won or placed second.

This national and international attention is a prize worth far more in publicity and a shot in the arm to the fundraising and recruitment of officeholders and activists than would be indicated by the miniscule delegate count from any vote here.

This publicity provides adrenaline for anyone who receives a first- or second-place finish (no one has done anything with a third-place performance); such winners discover that these magazine covers along with other favorable media exposure provide the necessary lift-off to enable the winners or close contenders to move on to the next stage with a more significant presence.

Also, officeholders and activists in both parties are alerted about who the real contenders are and can recognize the importance of deciding whom to support for the nomination before it is too late.

A victory here can often lead to the White House, as it did for General Dwight Eisenhower (who appeared on the cover of *Newsweek* on March 31, 1952), after defeating "Mr. Republican," Ohio senator Robert Taft by 10,823 votes in the first primary. Or it may fail even to lead to a presidential nomination—as the coonskin-capped Senator Estes Kefauver of Tennessee discovered after gracing the cover of *Time* on March 24, 1952, following his stunning upset of President Harry Truman by 3,873 votes in the March 11 Democratic primary.

Following his upset of former vice president Walter Mondale of Minnesota by 9,500 votes in the 1984 New Hampshire

Democratic presidential primary, Colorado senator Gary Hart
began a wave of media momentum seldom matched in American
political history.

Following the vote on February 28, by March 12 Hart was on
the covers of *Newsweek*, *Time*, *U.S. News and World Report*, and the
Washington Post National Weekly Edition.

Another measure of Hart's rise to national prominence was
that in the month prior to the New Hampshire decision he raised
only $987,000, but in the month following his stunning upset his
coffers increased by $8.2 million, according to records of the
Federal Election Commission.

Ohio senator John Glenn, who many thought would be the
main challenger to Mondale, was able to raise $3.4 million in the
month prior to the first primary, but following his third-place
showing with just 12% he could raise only $698,000, a decrease of
$2.8 million. Glenn would stay in the race through Super Tuesday
but he withdrew just three days after a poor showing.

Now, in an era of rapid technological change, there are new
ways to measure just how important a New Hampshire presidential primary win can be.

The morning following Senator John McCain's victory by
43,276 votes over George W. Bush, in the Feb. 14, 2000 issue of
Newsweek it was noted that by 7:30 A.M. $162,000 in contributions by
credit cards had been registered via the Web. *Newsweek* reported,

At the end of the week, campaign officials told
Newsweek, McCain2000.com had logged a staggering 10 million hits. More than $1.4 million in contributions poured in—
nearly as much money in three days as McCain had raised
over the Web in the previous nine months. The average take:
$119. Since contributions up to $250 are matched by the Feds,
McCain's total haul last week, thanks to the Internet, was
more than $2 million.

In 1992 New Hampshire lost its bellwether status, for those Independents and Democrats participating in the February 18 primary voted for former senator Paul Tsongas of Massachusetts by 14,123 votes over the eventual president—Arkansas governor Bill Clinton.

Of the 13 states that have held primaries continuously since 1952 this state was the last to fall from the category of perfect bellwether status. The previous one to fall was Pennsylvania, as its Republican primary provided an 8% win for George H. W. Bush in 1980 versus the next president—former California governor Ronald Reagan.

In the election in 1976 Oregon lost its perfect record when its Democratic voters decided by a margin of 7% to back Idaho senator Frank Church and not the former governor of Georgia, Jimmy Carter, who became the 39th president.

In 2000, for the second time in just three primaries, the Granite State failed to have the winner of the presidency first win here. Texas governor George Walker Bush, the son of the 41st president, lost to Arizona senator John McCain by an 18% margin—the greatest spread for a competitive GOP race here since 1980.

In the 13 primaries that have been held since 1952, three states have exceeded New Hampshire's outcomes that sent a candidate on the way to the presidency: Illinois, Oregon and Pennsylvania have all done it 12 times compared to New Hampshire's 11.

Illinois and Oregon share the lead at voting 21 times for the 26 nominees to win the Democratic or Republican nominations awarded since 1952. Pennsylvania has achieved this 20 times and the Granite State 17.

Since the first collection of presidential primaries was held in 1912 (12 that year) they have served time and time again as a device to open up a closed and often stagnant political system; indeed, the case can be made that the New Hampshire primary in 1968 has probably done more for this nation than any other such election.

The primaries often act as a ventilation system that permits the voting public (not just the political elite) to render a referendum on the nation's leaders and their policies.

Presidential primaries were an important component of the agenda of the progressive movement in this nation approximately a century ago. The objective was to restrict the flow of power into the hands of the party bosses and influential business groups and place it in the hands of the voting public.

According to *Presidential Elections Since 1798* (published by Congressional Quarterly in 1975), "Part of this 'return to the people' was the inauguration of primary elections, wherein candidates for office would be chosen by the voters of their party rather than by what were looked upon as boss-dominated conventions. It was only a matter of time before the idea spread from state and local elections to the presidential contests."

In 1968 the president, the Congress and even the federal judiciary managed to deal so poorly with the issue of the war in Vietnam that this conflict was becoming a crisis. The New Hampshire primary held on March 12 of that year resulted in a decision that became a referendum on that policy and managed to set in motion a chain of events that eventually led to a change of leadership and finally a change of direction for this nation.

Some might think it strange to select a primary that the challenger (Eugene McCarthy) to the write-in on behalf of President Lyndon Johnson lost by 4,251 votes. And who, after winning six primaries—Wisconsin, Pennsylvania, Massachusetts, Oregon, New Jersey and Illinois—still did not become the nominee. That honor went to Vice President Hubert Humphrey, who did not enter a single state primary.

Without the nomination McCarthy did not become president, and despite a great deal of pressure for him to enter the general election as a third-party candidate, in the end (on Oct. 29, to be exact) he endorsed his former colleague from Minnesota shortly before the election on Nov. 5 that was narrowly won by Richard Nixon.

However, the McCarthy campaign here (he announced his candidacy on Nov. 30, 1967), had a profound impact that helped lead to Robert Kennedy's entry on March 16, just four days after the New Hampshire result was in, to Johnson's withdrawal on March 31, and then to Humphrey's entrance on April 27. And it helped muster an eventual change in American foreign policy— first to de-escalation and eventually to withdrawal of our troops several years later from South Vietnam.

Surely many other primaries have had a significant impact on the direction of this nation—the 1952 and 1980 GOP primaries come to mind—but it is hard to argue against the contention that the 1968 New Hampshire Democratic presidential primary has had the greatest effect on this nation.

In one respect the impact of McCarthy's challenge to the political establishment is still felt to this day.

That change has helped to lead to the supremacy of the primary in the nomination process. And it has even forced the GOP to tag along with approximately the same number of primaries, although given the hierarchical nature of the Grand Old Party it is a far rarer occurrence to see grassroots efforts emerge like those that brought outsiders such as Jimmy Carter and to some extent Bill Clinton out of the Democratic pack and into the presidency.

In her book *Hart and Soul*, Susan Casey, co-director of the 1984 campaign for Gary Hart here, quoted the senator from Colorado at the end of the book as stating, "I think a campaign ought to be more than getting one person elected. I think a campaign ought to be a crusade. I think a campaign ought to be a great national referendum on the future of this democracy. I think a campaign ought to be a vehicle for involving American citizens in the determination of their own destiny."

Never more so than in 1968—in New Hampshire.

One of the most recent books written on the first primary was British scholar Niall Palmer's *New Hampshire Primary*. It concludes with this paragraph:

> New Hampshire's primary, at the forefront of the election calendar, has also been at the forefront of these battles and seems destined, during the 1980s, to become a major casualty. Its fate, however, remains closely linked to the tides of reform, and these tides are now following strongly in the Granite State's favor. The first-in-the-nation primary may be preserved; indeed, it must be preserved if the legend is to survive that all Americans, whatever their financial or political status, have a chance to be elected president of the United States.

One hopes that Palmer's optimistic view pans out, but it does swim against the tide of homogenization that has become so much the centerpiece of the American experience in the past several decades.

If one can now "enjoy" the same fast-food dining "experience" in Calais, Maine, as one can in San Diego, California, can a similar tide long be resisted in the menu of choices we are asked to select from every quadrennium in first nominating and finally electing our president?

Since we now have a process that can only be described as "of the consultants, by the consultants and for the consultants," will there remain for long a meaningful role for the Granite State as the first primary state?

As the calendar of caucuses and primaries becomes more and more frontloaded, how restricted will the opportunities be for the lesser known and underfunded hopefuls without a national identity to have any reasonable chance of enduring the first round of contests? Will they have the chance to join the process when the megastates quickly identify the nominees of each major party as their considerable delegate contingents are determined?

And what of a process that permits the grassroots to wither as the parties march toward the altar of television as the most significant (and most expensive) communications medium in determining who becomes a serious contender and who is shunted to the sidelines.

Time and again the argument has been made that the Granite State, first settled by Europeans in 1623 and one of the original 13 colonies, is not representative of the rest of the nation.

Leaving aside for now the question of what criteria should be utilized to anoint the most representative state to replace New Hampshire at the front of the presidential selection parade (and would those making the selection of a truly representative state be themselves representative of the nation?) once in a while an argument is made against this small state that can only leave one shaking one's head.

In the August/September 1975 issue of the short-lived publication *The Democratic Review*, Harold Wolff, its executive editor, wrote, "Clearly burdened by size in attempting to speak for the nation, New Hampshire also wins no prizes for representativeness. Neither its people nor their environment are similar to national profiles."

After citing statistics proving just how white, nonurban and below the national average in nonmanufacturing employment this state is, Wolff noted, "Its crime statistics are among the lowest in the nation. In incidents of robbery, for example, New Hampshire reports 13.3 cases per 100,000 residents compared to a national average of 182.4 per 100,000."

In the years since that was written, the state's eligibility for prizes for representativeness has not improved.

In the October 2001 *New Hampshire Economic Review*, published by Public Service Company of New Hampshire, the state's largest utility company, in a ranking of states according to the crime rate in 1999 (crimes per 100,000 population), the Granite State, with just 2,281.9 crimes per 100,000, is the lowest in the nation. Evidently based on this criterion Montana, with its 4,069.9 crimes per 100,000 (placing it 25th in the nation) is much better suited to become the first primary state.

Do the citizens of New Hampshire have to commit more crimes than they do at present in order to become more representative and therefore present a stronger case to retain this state's first direct vote in the nomination process?

As the 2004 presidential election grows closer, more attention will be centered on the nominating campaigns, in particular the initial stirrings in the state with the traditional first caucus (Iowa) and the first primary (New Hampshire).

Martin Gross was born in New York City in 1938. He received a bachelor's degree from Harvard in 1960 and a law degree from Harvard Law School in 1964. He began the practice of law the following year in the state capital in a firm that overlooks the State House plaza. Active in the Democratic Party for several decades, Gross has been a keen observer of all things political in his adopted state.

Asked his opinion about just how unrepresentative the first primary state is, he responded,

In some respects it's true, in other aspects it's not. In some respects we're nonrepresentative in very good ways. In some respects we're not representative in other ways. Sure, we don't have a major amount of poverty, we don't have major labor union clout; but we have people, particularly in the Democratic primary; we pay attention to what major candidates are saying and what it is they're trying to get across.

Frankly, the opportunity for a candidate to demonstrate that he or she has the ability to attract votes is very important and to me far outweighs the concept that perhaps the votes cast here are not quite representative. Representative of what?

This is a big country with a whole lot of different strains in it.

In order to assemble a consensus to get elected president of this country you've got to be able to attract a whole range of it and it doesn't trouble me that we may represent not the entire range of interests that characterize the political process, because I think we have something else to offer.

The Iowa decision is a relatively new phenomenon in American politics (the first time it received national attention was in 1972), but the New Hampshire primary has deep roots in our presidential nominating campaigns.

The Granite State has conducted a presidential primary since 1916 and it has been first-in-the-nation beginning in 1920. The reason for this is that Indiana decided after its March 7 primary in 1916 that this was far too early in the process, so it shifted back to the first Tuesday in May, allowing it to have a better understanding of how the nomination races were shaping up; and Minnesota, which had been with New Hampshire on the second Tuesday in March in 1916, reverted to the more traditional caucus format.

The Granite State is often attacked by political leaders, academics, late-night comedians, reporters and newspaper editors for being too unrepresentative, too small, lacking in sufficient minority population, and with one daily newspaper supposedly having too much influence.

New Hampshire has not been a failure as the first step in the actual voting for president, but in fact has been too successful.

The state has performed the role the progressives set out to accomplish when they advocated presidential primaries to permit a far larger constituency a voice in political parties' presidential nominations.

The publicity the Granite State has achieved has led to a New Hampshirization of the process, for more and more states have been shifting from caucuses to primary elections and many of these states have also shifted their primaries to an earlier date on the nomination calendar.

(It might come as a surprise to some that in manufacturing jobs as a percentage of population, in 2000 New Hampshire ranked 11th in the nation. This hardly squares with the rural and oh-so-bucolic portrait that is so often painted—particularly by visiting reporters.)

Given the small population of the Granite State (41st according to the 2000 census), the limited amount of money required to stump in a location that is also quite small (46th) in size and the fact that the state had only 46 of the 6,405 delegates to the last national nominating conventions means that New Hampshire can provide as level a playing field as one can find in this nation.

What this means is that not just the nationally known presidential contenders receive a hearing here. This state wedged into the top of northern New England between Maine and Vermont and below the province of Quebec, Canada, is one of the few places where candidates in the middle tier have a chance to step up to the microphone and state their cases to the rest of the nation.

Candidates from Tennessee senator Estes Kefauver in 1952 to Arizona senator John McCain in the last primary are just two who have found this state to be their lift-off to a national campaign, a platform that is unlikely to remain if a national or regional primary system is enacted.

Even the most zealous defenders of the lead-off primary can't use the total number of voters in the 13 primaries held since 1952 as any sort of defense for what transpires here. In the 2000 California Republican primary alone, 1,387,866 more people managed to vote than did in New Hampshire in the 13 primaries since 1952 for both parties.

Therefore the quantity of the vote can't be used in any way to defend the first primary state's role; there obviously have to be some other elements involved to explain why candidates and the media return here in such numbers every quadrennium.

The first primary state no longer maintains its perfect bell-wether status since in two of the last three elections the winner here did not win the White House; therefore, some will contend that the primary is no longer as important as it once was. Yet one would be disabused of that notion by tracking just how often aspirants to our highest office visit the state—often years in advance of the actual vote.

Over the past several decades the notice the Granite State has reaped has led to a determined attempt to reduce its influence by moving as many states as possible to the start of the nomination process. If this continues unabated, it will surely lead to a reduction of the impact this small state has had for so long.

If the attempt to reduce the disproportionate influence both Iowa and New Hampshire have enjoyed is maintained, it will lead to the creation of a de facto national primary, thus affecting our political process far more profoundly than having just two states adhere to their traditional positions.

You don't have to be a political scientist to figure out the linkage between the increasing influence of television in this nation's politics and the substantial decline in the vigor of our political parties.

If the latest version of Super Tuesday is finally transformed into some variation of National Primary Day, the role of television (both free and paid) in the campaign will be overwhelming, with an accompanying dilution of what little power the national and state parties retain.

A gradual and lengthy state-by-state process will become a mass media extravaganza and the already too long ordeal of a nomination campaign will give way to an even longer effort to raise sufficient funds to ensure a hopeful what will matter most—a well-funded TV blitz or personal bank account to buy enough air time on local television stations in our largest urban markets (for the campaigns often take longer than the time required to read a Russian novel).

In assessing what the problem with frontloading is, attorney Gross stated,

> It surely is a problem for candidates without any money because there's no time for them to gin up a campaign and run a national campaign and gear up at various times with various places. It all seems to be more and more geared to mass media and big money. If you don't have big money and you can't mount a mass-media campaign, you can't mount simultaneous campaigns in all these jurisdictions. The one good thing about that prolonged process that we used to have was that it was a longer horse race. Now everything happens in a big bang. . . . I believe that the result of compression of selection is simply to further magnify the role of money in this process which is already too big. . . . We see processes where candidates who have access to money and mass media tend to win. And others who can really radiate personally to people don't.

Once in a while someone does speak up for the nomination system. One such voice was columnist John F. Stacks, writing in *Time* magazine on March 21, 1988:

> For all its problems, the chaotic primary system has infused American politics with the life and energy it needs. The process offers unknowns a chance to shine in the early, small-state races. It permits the best organized and the best financed to show their stuff in Olympian contests like Super Tuesday. And although one can argue that money and TV advertising distorted last week's results, the ability to raise a lot of cash in small amounts from a lot of people is a kind of plebiscite in itself, a test of a candidate's core support. In its very complexity, the system tests those who would be President in many ways, most of which are relevant to the qualities necessary to be an effective President.

This small state has been described as "that magnetic collecting point for presidential candidates." And it has been the trigger for so many of the arguments as to what ails the nomination system.

Although virtually all the laws and regulations that exist today stem from actions by the two national parties, the state parties, and the 50 state legislatures, little action has been forthcoming from Congress.

This fact of life does not prevent numerous bills from being filed to change the system to a national primary, a series of regional primaries, or a system of four common dates that was the idea of Arizona congressman Morris Udall, who died on December 12, 1998.

If a system of regional primaries were established by Congress, just how often would an insurmountable advantage in terms of media coverage, organizational strength and fundraising be provided to aspirants from megastates versus those competing from states with far fewer residents and much smaller contributor bases?

However, there is one aspect of the first primary that does venture away from the level-playing-field concept: how well candidates from Massachusetts have performed when they've ventured over the border.

Sen. John Kennedy won the Democratic primary in 1960 without serious opposition. Ambassador to South Vietnam Henry Cabot Lodge won the GOP vote with a write-in in 1964. Gov. Michael Dukakis handily won the Democratic primary in 1988 and became the nominee. Former senator Paul Tsongas defeated Gov. Bill Clinton of Arkansas in the 1992 Democratic primary, which ended New Hampshire's streak extending back to 1952 of having the winner of the White House first win in the Granite State primary.

Only Sen. Edward Kennedy, who was defeated by President Carter in 1980, was a Bay Stater who lost a New Hampshire primary.

Obviously the role of the Boston media has been important in helping to provide generally positive play whenever one of their own has ventured north to press the flesh.

Yet the failure of Tsongas to win the nomination in 1992 or Dukakis the general election in 1988 might persuade the national press corps to examine why New Hampshire, with such obvious Frostbelt characteristics, has a voting outcome in the general election that almost always seems to follow the pattern of those voting in the Sunbelt.

Such an observation may not be good news for any future Democratic presidential hopefuls from one of the most liberal states in the nation who would attempt to use one of the most conservative ones as a launching pad to the White House.

In his column in the *Boston Globe* on April 24, 1988, Mike Barnicle wasn't shy about predicting the outcome of the general election six months hence. He wrote, "Memory reminded me how easily Mike Dukakis will beat George Bush this fall, and if you sit still for a moment I will tell you why," his lead read.

In the next-to-the-last paragraph Barnicle noted,

> While George Bush knows which spoon to use first during state dinners, Dukakis knows how to have him for breakfast. And if you think Dukakis is boring, he'll make Bush look and sound like a headstone three minutes into their first debate. Mark this down now: The race for president will be over by the first commercial break and Bush will spend October and November looking like a man in search of executive-size Pampers.

The election had a different outcome. Dukakis did carry 10 states (nine more than Walter Mondale achieved against President Ronald Reagan in 1984), but he managed to lose by 7 million votes. And the neighboring state that launched him onto the national stage on February 16, 1988, was not in his corner in November. In fact, the 63.2% that George H. W. Bush received here was his third highest tally of the vote of the two major parties—with his percentage lower only than Utah's 67.4% and Idaho's 63.3%, according to *Congressional Quarterly*.

The Granite State does have a Frostbelt climate. And any tour of the cities throughout the state would leave someone to conclude that the economy is industrially based, with so many mills and factories constructed alongside the rivers that such industry may well be all it has in common with the other states of New England and the Northeast. It certainly doesn't share a voting pattern. You can mark that down.

In gaining traction in the lead-off primary the way one builds an organization is crucial. Doubtless it is quite helpful to have in one's corner a major officeholder who can turn over his own organization to the candidate that organization has given its blessing.

Republican governors Sherman Adams (in 1952 for General Dwight Eisenhower) and John Sununu (in 1988 for Vice President George H. W. Bush) are classic examples of how to use an indigenous preexisting group to help someone to the White House: Both Adams and Sununu went on to serve as the top aide to the person he helped elect.

However, there are other varieties of indigenous organizational models. Three examples are Eugene McCarthy's bid in 1968, Gary Hart's in 1984 and John McCain's in 2000. These men all had to build from the bottom up, since there was no major officeholder in their corners. They were also considered long shots without any sort of national base so their national hierarchy was practically nonexistent.

Now in launching a national campaign this may not be such a liability, for this leaves the state campaigns free to craft the type of campaign the local organizations understand better than the

national campaign and therefore an effort that has the best chance
of catching fire.

Certainly the lack of resources from D.C. is a hindrance, but
the Granite State is, after all, a place with only 1.2 million residents
and still a low-budget entry point. It still does permit the grip-and-
grin approach along with town hall meetings and kaffeeklatsches
in living rooms, a campaign style that would have little impact in
a megastate.

In *Hart and Soul*, Casey provided an evaluation of what transpired in the Hart campaign of '84 and the interaction between the
New Hampshire and D.C. operations: "While tradition has it that
there are always conflicts between state campaigns and the
national office in presidential contests, that was not the case with
the Hart campaign. From the start there was a sense of cama-
raderie." Casey also wrote, "While there had been a lot of activity
in 1982 around a presidential bid, any resemblance to a strong or
deep national campaign structure with concrete plans was purely
accidental." This was a result of a lack of funds, but she also noted,
"According to Hart, if there had been a large and sophisticated
staff in Washington, there would have been no money for New
Hampshire, and he had always been a believer in grassroots politics and local autonomy."

There are other ways to approach this state. Just about everyone who has run from neighboring Massachusetts has used, to one
degree or another, the nearby remote control approach. This is a
situation where candidates such as Michael Dukakis in 1988 and
Paul Tsongas in 1992 simply utilized their national campaign staff
in Boston to direct their efforts in the first primary.

Then there is the remote control via Washington, D.C., model,
often resulting in a true organizational nightmare for all concerned. Here the president, a senator, or congressman hires a team
of campaign operatives not only to run the D.C. headquarters, but
also to actually attempt to execute a national campaign strategy.

That's when serious problems can result and possibly one critical reason so few sitting United States senators ever make it to the Oval Office.

Former governor (1953–1955) Hugh Gregg offered this advice in the documentary program "The Premier Primary" produced by John Gfroerer:

> Well, the first thing you do when you come into New Hampshire is you get rid of all your Washington advisers. That's the first thing you do.
>
> Because every candidate that comes in here comes in with a book of directions from somebody in Washington—some professional group or, if they've been in the White House, they're White House people—that tell you how to run a campaign in New Hampshire. So that's the first thing you do—you get rid of those people.

These campaign staffers almost always come to the conclusion that the Hawkeye State is just as important (if not more so) than the Granite State, even though a simple study of election returns would indicate that simply isn't so.

Then there is the organizational model that could be called remote control with nobody home. That was the effort for President Gerald Ford versus former California governor Ronald Reagan—who had the vigorous support of the *Manchester Union Leader*.

In launching the Ford primary campaign his Granite State backers were hampered by the lack of any sort of direction from the national campaign headquarters. Requests for campaign materials or information went unheeded. Miles of red tape were necessary for approval to distribute a White House press release.

The campaign manager here was John Michels, who had served two terms in the New Hampshire House, winning his first election in 1968 with a mail campaign while serving in the Army in South Vietnam.

Michels stated, "You couldn't get a thing approved. Even a press release from the White House—we couldn't get it. 'Oh my God, we've got to get a new set of approvals to do so.' They just didn't know what the world was like out there."

The campaign got off to a poor start, largely due to the absence of an overall plan and the fact that the campaign organizers operated on the false assumption that since very other president had had an organization, Ford did too. Big mistake. Michels said,

> Gerald Ford didn't have an organization. The national campaign didn't know what they wanted to do here. After a while we did things here regardless of what anybody said in Washington. They wouldn't decide on anything. So we just went out and did things. The people in Washington just never got their act together.
>
> I always had the feeling that the people in the White House and the Washington headquarters had no comprehension of what the world was about because they were so removed from everything. I didn't feel our enemy was Reagan as much as it was our people in Washington.

Despite all this, Ford did eke out a victory—by just 1,587 votes, the closest primary victory on record here.

The national campaign headquarters always has control over the schedule of the candidate and the budget. Even though the first primary state is a lot closer to D.C. than, say, Idaho or Oregon, getting the candidate to allot sufficient time to meet and greet the proper number of activists and the voting public is never easy.

Further complicating the organizational flow out of D.C. is that sometimes even the national campaign isn't given free rein over the direction of the effort. Every senator or congressman not only has his or her own staff, but also advisers, consultants, friends and family members who all are involved to some extent in the organization, adding yet another level of frustration for the folks laboring away out in the countryside.

Prior to becoming president, Jimmy Carter, Bill Clinton and George W. Bush maintained their national headquarters in Atlanta, Little Rock and Austin respectively. That may be one reason all three made it to the White House and no senator or congressman did during these elections.

Perhaps the most salient statement as to why the Senate of the United States is not much of a launching pad to the presidency was written by Arthur Hadley in his 1976 book, *The Invisible Primary*: "The Senate—there is no way around the fact—at present provides dangerously little training for the presidency. Indeed cocooning a man inside an expensive club it may be a handicap."

In a rather prescient comment in *USA Today* on February 5, 1988 (just three days before the Iowa caucus), former vice president Walter Mondale stated, "When you win in Iowa, I think the voters of New Hampshire want to turn you down and pick the president; they don't want Iowa to do it. If Richard Gephardt wins Iowa, Michael Dukakis will win New Hampshire; if Robert Dole wins Iowa, George Bush will win New Hampshire."

And that is what happened. The Iowa caucus has grown in significance so that in some years it seems to outshine the first primary. Much of the reason for that can be traced to the news media, for it was, after all, ABC News director of political operations Stan Opotowsky who was quoted in *Newsweek* boasting, "We made Iowa into a primary."

In *The Iowa Precinct Caucuses*, published in 1987, author Hugh Winebrenner noted,

The news trendsetters—the *New York Times* and the *Washington Post*—were among those who "discovered" the precinct caucuses, and they pointed the way to Iowa in 1976 for political reporters embarrassed by their errors of judgment in the 1972 Muskie–McGovern race. One reporter, R. W. Apple of the *New York Times*, probably deserves the title of Father of the Iowa Media Event for focusing media attention on the local meetings. His stories about the 1972 outcomes and the surprisingly strong McGovern finish, and his stories about the 1976 Jefferson–Jackson Day preference poll, in which he alerted the nation to the strong Carter campaign in Iowa, may have legitimized the precinct caucuses as a source of hard news for the news media.

A strange thing often happens on the way to the coronation of our version of a king every quadrennium: The voters here have this bad habit of overturning the Iowa decision and rendering their own at the top of northern New England.

Mondale was partly right about the desire of Granite Staters to "pick the president." What the results here usually mean is that rather than shutting down the contest after just two states have been heard from, the script the national news media attempt to hand down to the lumpen proletariat is instead sent to rewrite. Hence this pattern of having the first two contests have different outcomes means that the race for the nomination is opened up— rather than closed down—providing voters in a number of other states a say in the process of choosing the presidential nominee.

So instead of a situation where two supposedly unrepresentative states disenfranchise the rest of the nation, New Hampshire's contrary-minded pattern of voting behavior ensures that a number of other states will have some relevance—and once again the national news media are put in their places and told not to call the race until far more voters have been heard from.

It seemed to this observer in watching the TV coverage in the last presidential campaign before the vote in Iowa on January 24 and New Hampshire on February 1, that only ABC in its news coverage managed to grasp this concept. And of all the presidential candidates since Iowa came onto the national stage only Sen. John McCain of Arizona managed to craft a strategy to bypass the first caucus and still win the first primary—thus validating the concept that the much ballyhooed Iowa bounce is nothing more than a hiccup.

When interviewed for my book *First in the Nation*, Joanne Symons, the Second District coordinator for Morris Udall's bid in 1976, traced the reason for his defeat here:

> The problem was Iowa. That was the worst decision that was made by his staff in Washington. That he ever bothered to go there, when Jimmy Carter had been there for a year, was stupid. And that he spent badly needed money in Iowa and, more important, valuable time. We were all screaming, "What's he doing in Iowa? Get him back here because we can win here." It was really going those last two months. We were beside ourselves—my God, we might win. If he'd won here, if he'd beaten Jimmy Carter, I think Carter would have been dead—I really do.

The problem with Iowa is its size. With 56,276 square miles it is far too large—26th in the nation in terms of size. It has a population of 2.9 million, ranked 30th in the nation in this category.

There are merits to the caucus system that just a handful of states (only 16 in the last presidential race) still retain. But the physical test a candidate confronts should be a reasonable one. Should anyone have to spend 129 days, as Representative Richard Gephardt did in the Hawkeye State prior to winning the vote in 1988?

Iowa would also be a more reasonable organizational test for presidential wannabes if a change were made. It simply makes no sense to use television to communicate with such a limited electorate in caucuses held in the dead of winter on a Monday evening. If candidates would come to their senses and realize they are spending hundreds of thousands of dollars for no reason whatsoever, they would make tremendous strides toward improving the process and the value of this first test.

No doubt the television stations that benefit from such outlays and the political consultants who receive each quadrennium such a windfall (usually 15% of the ad buy), would scream, but they won't go broke and there would still be a plethora of other ways to spend campaign funds.

Would such a change lower the level of attention this state receives? I doubt it. Does anyone really think that foregoing TV ads in the first caucus state would lead to the disappearance of the hopefuls from the Iowa landscape? And would the demise of the Iowa GOP straw poll cause any harm to our democracy?

Political punditry seems to say that once the Iowa outcome is determined the rest simply falls into place; that is, Iowa begets New Hampshire and this state in turn determines what happens in South Carolina and so on down the line.

Repeated often enough it has the resonance of truth, but an examination of the record shows it just isn't so.

Back in early 1988, just a few weeks prior to the Iowa vote and with the Granite State test to follow just eight days later, I was having lunch in Concord with a political columnist. He was of the opinion that once the Iowa caucus was held New Hampshire would certainly follow the Iowa returns. I recall his observation that once about a dozen or so analysts such as he determined what the returns from the first caucus state meant, they could predict to a great degree what would happen in the next election. I disagreed and said the world (especially the part of it New Hampshire occupies) doesn't work that way.

The 1988 winners in Iowa—Gephardt for the Democrats and

Bob Dole for the Republicans—not only failed to see any bounce to win the Granite State, but by Super Tuesday Gephardt had won only his home state of Missouri (he dropped out by March 28) and Dole was shut out on Super Tuesday (he left the day after). So much for the value of all the spin coming out of the cornfields of Iowa.

Al Gore's narrow primary win here in 2000 over Bill Bradley meant that for the first time in two decades a winner in the first caucus also won the first primary. (President Jimmy Carter defeated Ted Kennedy in both contests in 1980). Obviously, reporters should be primed for another occurrence of the much ballyhooed Iowa bounce in the year 2020. Maybe by then the GOP winner in Iowa will also have won in New Hampshire for the very first time.

Critics of Iowa's and New Hampshire's inordinate amount of influence frequently recommend a series of rotating regional primaries (ranging in number from five to seven) as the best corrective measure. On occasion some cite the need for a national primary.

Surely with millions voting on a single day a national primary would serve as a far more democratic model for the nomination system than what exists today. Or would it?

Would more democracy prove in the end to be more democratic? In the Feb. 1, 1988 issue of *Newsweek*, Sen. Daniel Moynihan of New York (who died on March 26, 2003) wrote, "Only the innocent assume that the more persons who are involved in a process, the more democratic it is. Power gravitates to the special and the organized, as against the general interest."

Generally there are three major components that have standing in the nomination process. One is the political leadership, both within Washington, D.C., and without; another is the news media, not just the network and cable news organizations and major newspapers; the third is the general public, at least those who take the time to assist a campaign and vote in a caucus or primary and then do the same in the general election.

Much like the construction in our federal Constitution with a system of judicial, executive and legislative branches, the ad hoc arrangement of the three major spheres of influence in the nomination process seems to work best when there is a balance among these three elements.

However, would a new arrangement with a national or series of regional primaries still be in balance? Would not such a revision lead to an enormous shift in clout to the news media—not just to the national broadcast and cable networks but to the television stations and daily newspapers in the major cities of this nation?

With such a change would the candidates without a national power base have any way to raise their recognition level if they haven't been deemed the frontrunner by the media or if they lack the personal wealth of a Nelson Rockefeller, a Steve Forbes or a Ross Perot?

What chance will they have to make it all the way to the Oval Office if they lack the resources to make a credible challenge beyond just a few states? In other words, what chance would someone without great wealth or a base in a megastate have to step up to the microphone and state his or her case to a national audience?

The first primary state has passed through three phases in the half-century of its existence as a complete election.

From 1952 to 1972 the primary was embraced by many a news media operation; it was, after all, the *New York Times* that printed a complete page of editorial comment from 43 newspapers after the candidate so dear to its heart—General Dwight Eisenhower—won here with 50.2% of the GOP vote.

It wasn't until Florida in 1972 decided to hold its primary on the same day as New Hampshire's that this state for the first time had to advance its primary from the second Tuesday in March, where it had been since 1916.

It was in 1972 that Senator Edmund Muskie of Maine had his infamous emotional scene in front of William Loeb's *Manchester Union Leader* on a snowy Saturday morning just 10 days before the vote—a test Muskie still won by 8,278 votes over Senator George McGovern of South Dakota.

Since the controversy surrounding New Hampshire's prominence was as thick as the snow at the Muskie event, the state soon had more than Florida to worry about.

By 1976 an effort was made to construct a New England regional primary. This effort was led by political operative Mark Shields and then Bay State state representative Barney Frank, who won the 5th congressional district in 1980 and still serves in the U.S. House of Representatives. But just Massachusetts and Vermont joined in, an indication that some of the states of this region can be as independent as their residents.

By 1980 the first step toward a Southern regional primary was taken when Florida, Georgia and Alabama all voted on March 11. Thus began the effort to construct a massive Super Tuesday vote to act in part as a counterweight for Southern aspirants who were having trouble gaining traction in Iowa and New Hampshire after Jimmy Carter left the White House.

After the flop that Super Tuesday (a.k.a. Stupid Tuesday) turned out to be in 1988 when political leaders and reporters learned just how difficult it was to campaign in and cover an election in 20 states in a single day, the small state of New Hampshire, although still not popular with all, seems to have regained some stature—enough at least to continue to fend off attempts to chase it from its initial primary perch.

Without any doubt the victory here in the 1996 GOP primary by conservative commentator Pat Buchanan did not do much to enhance the state's reputation, especially among the national Republican establishment and the Republican National Committee, the organization responsible for setting that party's nomination rules.

The Granite State was the only primary Buchanan managed to carry in his bids in 1992 and 1996, something that can be used as evidence of just how far out of the mainstream this state is.

Lost in the discussion of how conservative the Granite State can be is the fact that the following states in 1996 provided a higher percentage of votes than the 27.2% Buchanan managed with his win here. Those states were Arizona (27.6%), South Dakota (28.6%), South Carolina (29.2%), Georgia (29.1%), Louisiana (33.1%), Michigan (33.9%) and Wisconsin (33.8%).

Buchanan had a base of just above a quarter of the vote, but he could win only while candidates such as former governor of Tennessee Lamar Alexander and Sen. Richard Lugar of Indiana were crowding Kansas senator Bob Dole. Once Alexander and Lugar dropped out on the same day (March 6), Dole had the moderate GOP base to himself.

This was not the first time a division of the moderate vote had helped determine the outcome of the lead-off primary. In 1980 the vote percentage of Illinois congressman Phil Crane, Texan John Connally and Bob Dole (then considered a conservative) amounted to just 3.7%. By contrast, George H. W. Bush had to fight for a moderate base and saw 12.9% go to Tennessee senator Howard Baker and 9.9% to Illinois congressman John Anderson. Therefore the Reagan win probably had more to do with the others competing than with who paid for what microphone in Nashua for the Saturday night "debate" prior to the vote.

The first period, 1952–1972, could be called the embrace phase, for in those two decades the state certainly generated a great deal of favorable press. The second phase—the rejection period—from 1972 to 1988—was when the national and regional press found it difficult to say or write anything positive about the first primary; "credit" for this belongs largely to one William Loeb.

In the third period—the acceptance phase—which began after Super Tuesday—the only irritant has been during the last two primaries Delaware's attempt to encroach on the Granite State. With Delaware's 784,000 residents (47th in the nation), in both 1996 and 2000 the first primary state has had to wage a lobbying and public relations offensive to keep all major candidates save Steve Forbes from waging any sort of effort in what some citizens of this state regard as the usurper state.

Delaware's attempts to hold a primary on the Saturday following the first primary on Tuesday comes in conflict with the law passed in 1995, which calls for a vote "on the second Tuesday in March or on a Tuesday selected by the secretary of state which is 7 days or more immediately preceding the date on which any other state shall hold a similar election, whichever is earlier, of each year when a president of the United States is to be elected or the year previous." Therefore there has been some degree of conflict between these two small states on the eastern seaboard.

Since Delaware is 74.6% white (and 19.2% black) it is a more diverse state than lily-white New Hampshire. Just how white is the first primary state? It isn't the whitest in the land; its 96% trails Maine's 96.9% and Vermont's 96.85%, according to the latest census. (Iowa is the fifth whitest at 93.9% and New Hampshire has an African American population of just 0.7%).

Obviously, if a major criterion of a state's value in such an important position at the start of the nomination parade is tied to how diverse the population is, both the Hawkeye (2.1% African American) and Granite states fail that test. (The national average for whites is 75.1%, Hispanics, 12.5% and African Americans, 12.3%.)

Yet if even one megastate were to serve instead in the first primary spot, would the process be that much better? Given the enormous populations of California with almost 34 million, Texas with 21 million, and New York with 19 million, would there be any chance for hopefuls other than those already nationally known such as Mario Cuomo, George W. Bush or Ronald Reagan to rise

out of the pack of contenders and step up to the podium to state
their cases as to why they should be the next president?

Given the enormous costs of paid advertising and the restric-
tions the major media tend to impose on covering all but a few of
the major contenders, what chance would an unknown such as a
John McCain, Gary Hart, George H. W. Bush (circa 1980) or Jimmy
Carter have to step onto the national stage?

Michael Birkner served as the editorial page editor and chief
editorial writer for the *Concord Monitor*, the liberal morning daily
based in this state's capital, with a circulation of 21,000, from 1983
to 1985. Now a professor at Gettysburg College in Pennsylvania,
he said of the first primary,

> I think that the size of the state, its traditions, the fact that
> it has been important historically has made people in New
> Hampshire a little more sensitive to their citizenship, and they
> take some pride—I really feel that New Hampshire people—
> not *all* by the way—take some pride in following the primary
> and voting in it.
>
> The majority of people go about their business and ignore
> the primary. I do think though [that] compared to
> Pennsylvania, compared to Maryland, compared to New
> Jersey or other states, this is a model of democracy in terms of
> people paying attention. You've got to think of it compara-
> tively. There is a total disconnect with the presidential primary
> system in places like Pennsylvania, because there is no way
> you can have the kind of citizen contact with candidates that
> you can have here.

Watching and reading the reporting of the nation's first vote
every leap year is difficult. No one can keep up with the quantity
of the work, and the quality of what is seen, read and heard often
leaves a great deal to be desired.

Much of the blame for this can be laid at the door of the national press corps, but some of it can be traced closer to home.

There are after all a number of histories of the state that was the 9th to ratify the U.S. Constitution on June 21, 1788, thus putting the Constitution into legal force, ahead of Virginia's vote by just four days.

However, there is a rather monotonous quality to these works, tracing time and again the initial settlement of Europeans in a small colony at the mouth of the Piscataqua River in 1623 to then moving inland and developing a colony and then a state.

What is sadly evident is that in the post–World War II period, a time span of just under six decades and what is surely a period of the most profound change this state has ever seen, is that there is no contemporary history to read and study.

Therefore the visiting press can cop a plea for their lack of understanding of the state while trying to piece together information from a variety of sources and now also the Internet.

There are works to study such as the *Almanac of American Politics* published every election year, but it is rather sad that one has to refer to a book published more than a quarter of a century ago when asked what sources to study to find out what makes the Granite State tick. That work is *The New England States*, published in the bicentennial year of 1976 by Norton and written by Neal Peirce.

Peirce, who picked up where the noted author John Gunther left off with his *Inside U.S.A.*, wrote this book as part of a 10-book series on this nation's states which culminated in *The Book of America: Inside 50 States Today*, published in 1983, also by Norton.

What distinguishes Peirce's work is that rather than what could be described as typed tantrums disguised as a newspaper column that one Michael Barnicle filed for the *Boston Globe* until his forced departure in 1998, Peirce does his homework. The depth and texture of his writing is rarely found elsewhere among those who tackle the subject matter that is the Granite State.

Also, the energy of his writing puts to shame so much that is written by those more content to pick up a paycheck with as little effort as possible. He just keeps digging and digging to uncover the truth about the subject matter he has decided to cover.

Peirce has a fondness for New England which was captured in the opening paragraph of his 1976 book:

> To return to New England and her mist-shrouded coast, her forested mountains, her Plymouth and Boston and town meeting villages, is like undertaking a voyage backward through time and history to the American touchstone.
>
> In many senses, New England is to America what Old England is to the English-speaking world: the womb and starting place; the fountainhead of a culture's language, law, and learning; the smaller geographic entity from which great spaces were colonized.

Peirce's roots extend into this state, for, as he wrote, "Since earliest childhood days, those magical words [New Hampshire!] have also meant for me a lake clear and deep, ringed by mountains, and a bright cottage by the water that will always be more home than any other place on earth."

Peirce was interviewed on a hot and humid late summer day in September 2002 on the deck of that cottage overlooking what many consider to be one of the state's more scenic lakes, Newfound, where Peirce's Boston grandfather first rented the cottage in 1902 and purchased it in 1907, where his grandson began his visits at the age of six months in 1932 and where, with his wife, Barbara, Peirce spends the months of June through October. This 1954 Princeton graduate was asked some questions concerning the primary. After all, in his 76-page chapter on this state, he labeled the section on the primary an "Exercise in Perversity."

Peirce:

> I reread what I wrote and it's a little harsh—actually the surprises that keep coming out have their own charm and value—upsetting value to what are presumed to be the way every pundit says it's going to go. So the contrary nature of the primary seems to appeal to me more and more as time goes on. It upsets applecarts. It doesn't do what people expect. . . . One of the charms of the New Hampshire primary, which I don't write about much in my book, has been the sort of mixing with very common, ordinary folks in rural and small-town settings, which I think is a good experience for a candidate. All of American politics is having that media jump.

In analyzing the grassroots campaign mode that still exists here versus what takes place in the media-rich megastates he has written a great deal about, Peirce observed,

> It's just that everything is so contrived. Candidates seem so much less willing to be themselves. Look at the last presidential election: Both Bush and Gore were talking about very marginal issues defined by the consultants as what small groups of swing voters were responding to, rather than what was on most people's minds, most people's concerns. You keep waiting for people to really say what they think and really be themselves and you so often don't see that. . . . They really don't let the candidates be the people they are or would like to be.

Unlike a great number of those who have written about the Granite State, including most of its historians, Peirce has a rather direct and blunt manner in his evaluation. For example, in *The New England States* he wrote,

> But compared to most of the other 13 original states, New

Hampshire offers a strikingly undistinguished history and tradition. One reads and rereads the state's history in search of great leaders and finds embarrassingly few; one looks for an important tradition in literature, the arts, or public policy and finds practically none; one tries to detect a sense of historic mission and is disappointed again.

The phrase "a miniscule primary electorate quite unrepresentative of the nation at large—demographically and attitudinally" was read back to the author 26 years after being published and received this reaction: "It's sort of an extreme statement I must confess and it's not as miniscule as it used to be since your population has grown by such leaps and bounds since World War II."

Peirce's book also quoted an anonymous former governor saying, " 'Making state government responsive is a task which the people of New Hampshire have not had the political intelligence to face up to.' It was the severest indictment that I have ever heard a U.S. governor, past or present, make about his state."

Questioned as to who made that remark, Peirce answered, "He's left this mortal coil. Sherman Adams told me that."

Since he occupied such a prominent and powerful position as publisher of the state's largest newspaper for three and a half decades, did William Loeb deserve the blame for the state's having such a deficiency in its "historic mission"? The author proclaimed, "He certainly set the tone for a lot of public life and discussion in New Hampshire for many decades."

The political editor for *Congressional Quarterly* from 1960 to 1969, Peirce was a founder in 1969 of *National Journal*, a publication which he also wrote for until 1997. With Curtis Johnson he coauthored the *Citistates Reports*, concerning compelling issues of metropolitan futures for newspapers in almost two dozen regions across the United States. He was also the lead author for the 1993 book *Citistates*.

In his book on this region Peirce managed to categorize the Grand Old Party in this state into three groups: those of the Gilded Age; the reformers that formed around 1910; "and finally the school of snarling conservatives, running from Styles Bridges to Meldrim Thomson, obsessed with Communist witch-hunting (an idea laughed out of court in Vermont) and fighting progressive taxation as though it were a plague."

Neal Peirce may have softened on the value of the nation's first primary, but the same can't be said of the taxophobic element that continues to guarantee that this is the only state in the Union never to have enacted a general sales or income tax.

Peirce observed,

> If the whole focus of a state is whether you take the pledge [a reference to the promise most gubernatorial candidates take to veto any broad-based tax and not a reference to the pledge of allegiance] or not—year in and year out—in many states people are willing to make the argument for what public serv-ices can create for people. But here if you begin to do that too much why suddenly you're for a broad-based tax and I just think that creates an attitude towards government that is overly hostile. . . . Government is us and government is a mutual enterprise that does many things that are vital to all of us. So there needs to be a balance in here. If you're over-whelming attitudinally—your whole life is focused on "no broad-based tax—don't let it get me"—I don't think that the set-up is conducive to balanced political thinking.

The prolific writer did acknowledge about his chapter on the Granite State, "There was this assumption a lot of government was—is a good idea—and I really don't believe that so much any-more. I believe that a lot of responsive government—to keep con-trol of—is a good idea."

Shortly after former vice president Dan Quayle dropped out of the race on Sept. 27, 1999, I recall hearing some analysis that even if he managed to emerge victorious in the first primary state, the way the nomination process is now constructed with front-loading as its defining feature, there was simply no chance for someone other than the frontrunner (George W. Bush in 2000) to utilize such a victory to advance to the nomination.

Now there was very little chance that Quayle would have emerged victorious here even with the support of former governor John H. Sununu, who was given so much credit for George Bush's win here after his third-place finish in Iowa in 1988.

In the end this reading of the situation proved quite prescient, for if you substitute the name McCain for Quayle you have to conclude that no matter who won the primary—if his name wasn't George Walker Bush with his incredible campaign treasury and the nearly complete lock on the GOP establishment—no matter how much of a bounce the victor in New Hampshire reaped, it wouldn't be enough for a ticket to give the acceptance speech in Philadelphia on the evening of Aug. 3, 2000.

One of the more interesting aspects of living in the first primary (as well as the first caucus) state is an opportunity to get to know the candidates that is unlike anywhere else in the nation.

Having a candidate stop by for a kaffeeklatsch at your home or in the neighborhood just doesn't happen that much in Miami, Chicago or Los Angeles. Having a candidate stay for an evening in your home just doesn't seem to take place that often in Phoenix, Denver or Atlanta.

Getting involved with the core group of supporters to begin to construct a statewide organization provides access to not just the candidate and his family but also his national staff and some supporters who travel here from other states, as well as on occasion prominent political leaders and celebrity supporters.

That core group of a couple dozen activists is crucial, for not much can be done in effective city-by-city and town-by-town organizing without a group with the right combination of experience and energy trying many ways to accomplish one thing—to win the nation's first direct vote for president every leap year, or come close to doing so.

Yet even if you do accomplish great things here you had better lay the groundwork elsewhere, for, as Estes Kefauver in 1952, Gary Hart in 1984, Pat Buchanan in 1996 and John McCain in 2000 all learned, a slingshot can take you only so far.

As Pat Buchanan was on the verge of winning the 1996 primary here I was called by several reporters and asked just what this meant down the road.

My observation was that even with his victory here, despite all the media attention and a larger campaign treasury, the media-centered effort by this conservative commentator would not result in as much of a bounce as it had for others in the past.

Buchanan completely lacked the ability to build a strong national organization to take advantage of his upset of Bob Dole. In addition, he had no chance of winning over GOP major office-holders as Bob Dole had done, for these leaders matter a great deal in the remaining primaries and caucuses when time is far too short to try to construct the grassroots organizations that have to be erected in the first two traditional contests.

These leaders in both parties come to the forefront and if a possible president hasn't done the groundwork over prior years and decades, that strength coming out of Iowa and New Hampshire will dissipate just as the coastal fog does.

The earlier a candidate comprehends this, the more time he and his strategists have to develop a plan, so that when the time is right his campaign doesn't become a one-primary wonder—as Pat Buchanan learned to his dismay when he won just one of the primaries held in 1992 and 1996.

If asked in private conversation in the year 1983 (Gary Hart) and 1991 (Bill Clinton) as they began their efforts, whether their strongest backers had concerns about the marital fidelity of each, even if the answer had been yes, it's doubtful that many would have jettisoned either candidate.

Both men had a grasp of the issues, campaign abilities, and personal qualities that drew activists toward them.

Also, the alternatives weren't so compelling, since some others had questions in their private lives that could spill over into the headlines as they did for Hart and Clinton, and some had marginal qualities as leaders and campaigners.

In the early part of 1992, as allegations of adultery and draft-dodging by Governor Clinton surfaced, it was interesting that the outcome was different from what happened to Gary Hart when he was faced with his scandal involving Donna Rice.

When Gennifer Flowers strode into the Waldorf-Astoria in New York City on Jan. 27, 1992, after her charges of a 12-year affair were aired, the cable networks were full of pundits burying the Arkansas governor. After what happened to Hart the observations appeared to be correct.

However, the next day, as Clinton traveled to Austin to collect the endorsements of a good number of Texas Democratic leaders (when that state still had such a species), a good many of that state's Democratic establishment lined up behind him for the photo op. One could sense that this scandal might have a different outcome from Hart's.

Such a sight never occurred with Hart, for he was such a loner that it is doubtful that such a testimonial of support was possible even in his home state of Colorado.

Political leaders and activists here have an opportunity to get to know and understand the candidates, particularly since the primary campaign is now a permanent part of the process. With such lengthy campaigns now in vogue these supporters have just as much of an opportunity to learn what makes these men tick as the party bosses of yesteryear had.

We are a very long way from having Sen. Robert Taft of Ohio devote just three days in the last week of the 1952 primary to his campaign for votes here. Instead you have Pat Buchanan visiting for 109 days prior to the 1996 vote and Pierre du Pont IV devoting 93 days on his way to an anemic fifth-place finish in 1988.

So much time for the "getting to know you" phase is clearly ample for individuals here and in Iowa to really know these would-be presidents, even to begin to grasp what kind of character they have.

Character isn't the only part of their makeup to be evaluated, and character itself is a rather complex matter to consider.

Michael Birkner, now a professor of history at Gettysburg College says,

> How important is character to determine whether a person is going to be a worthy president? I don't think there's a right answer and wrong answer to that. I think character helps but it probably doesn't help as much as people think it does, 'cause Clinton had a lousy character but at least he was a decent president. Franklin Roosevelt didn't have a particularly good character but he was a great president. And we've had presidents like Hoover and Carter who were (of) exemplary character who weren't very good presidents.

The individual who managed to win the first primary more often than anyone else was none other than Richard Milhous Nixon. He did it three times—in 1960, 1968 and 1972. Since he was the only president to resign from office he surely fits into the character deficient "class" of presidents.

This fact is certainly Exhibit A that this state has not made perfect picks for president. But would the results have been that much better if one of the four largest states—California, Texas, New York or Florida—had had the first-in-the-nation presidential primary since 1952?

II

AN INVERTED BANANNA REPUBLIC

The truth was, most newspapermen—even many who had hated and assailed him—were sorry to see Hearst go because a great, violent, fascinating chunk of life and news went with him. He was an original, unique, so unusual that no one was even remotely like him, the newsiest figure in the whole world of news, simultaneously the Sphinx and the blabbermouth of journalism. His passing left the scene strangely sedate and dull.

— W. A. Swanberg, *Citizen Hearst*

ALSO IN THE BOOK *CITIZEN HEARST*, published in 1961, the author quoted the prime minister of Spain speaking to an American correspondent: "The newspapers of your country seem to be more powerful than the government."

It would not be an exaggeration to proclaim that in this state the *Union Leader is* the government. (The name was changed from the *Manchester Union Leader* in 1982.) There are often times when the state takes on the quality of an inverted Banana Republic, for it can seem that the state's largest daily and only statewide newspaper is in firm control of state government.

(In the interest of full disclosure, I acknowledge that I was hired by the Union Leader Corporation to write a brief history titled *First Primary: Presidential Politics in New Hampshire*, published in 1987.)

For the most recent case study of how conservative New Hampshire can be, you can examine the results of the last presidential contest. In November 2000 New Hampshire was the only state in the northeastern region of the nation to go Republican, with Governor George W. Bush of Texas winning by just 7,211 votes versus Vice President Al Gore; the state's four electoral votes provided Bush with the winning margin of three electoral votes.

In "Letter from New Hampshire" in the Jan. 31, 2000, issue of *The New Yorker*, author Hendrik Hertzberg's lead was:

> The Wayfarer Inn, in Bedford, just south of Manchester, is the unofficial headquarters of the New Hampshire primary. Every four years, as winter approaches, the Wayfarer begins to fill up with the camp followers of national politics: advance people, consultants, television technicians, political reporters and pundits, gofers, campaign staffers—even, sometimes, actual candidates and their entourages.

Quadrennium in and quadrennium out there always seems to be one topic rising above all others in the bar and restaurant of the Wayfarer. That topic is the *Union Leader*. Clearly, after Loeb's demise at the Lahey Clinic in Burlington, Massachusetts, the paper lost much of its vitriolic, strident advocacy for everything conservative, as well as some of its editorial punch.

(After his death Loeb's widow, Nackey, became the president and publisher of both newspapers and served in that capacity until May 14, 1999. She died in her home in Goffstown on Jan. 8, 2000.)

Yet it remains the newspaper of record for the state and it provides far more political coverage than any other. Although it now has to share the title of king of media hill with Channel 9, also based in the Queen City, it still deserves the credit or blame for this state's pronounced conservatism.

Much of the reason for this fixation was William Loeb, who had a unique ability to pull the chain of the national press corps whenever they'd invade the state to cover a presidential visit, a campaign swing by a presidential aspirant, or during the final weeks before the primary.

These journalists have always been primed to write yet again about the inordinate influence of this daily and Loeb's editorial posturing would often be reflected in the countless stories filed. However, after a study of the track record of this newspaper, you'd wonder why so many reporters have devoted so much attention to it.

The legacy of *Union Leader* publisher William Loeb carries on to this day (he succumbed to cancer on Sept. 13, 1981), for the Granite State is still the only one in the nation never to have enacted a general sales or income tax—a true reflection of its minimalist approach to governance. This embrace of limited government means that the first primary state has more in common with states in the South and West than it does with other northeastern states.

If there is a key to understanding Loeb and the power he was able to wield in this state, it is how rooted in the West—and not the East—he was. Once that is understood the rest falls into place.

In a letter to Sen. Styles Bridges that was published in the *New Hampshire Times* on April 27, 1977, Loeb wrote,

> Nackey and I continue to enjoy life in Nevada. We find ourselves very much in harmony with the thinking of Nevadans, especially the leaders of the state. These have no use for Eisenhower or Truman. They are real Americans and speak out bluntly and frankly, as I do, without this pussyfooting that has become so fashionable.

As an indicator of how harmonious the Granite State is with states in the South and West that also embrace the concept of small government more than their counterparts in the East, in fiscal 1999 New Hampshire was ranked lowest in state and local government tax burden in the country. Nevada was seventh.

Although publisher Loeb lived part of the year in his 30-room Tudor-style mansion in Prides Crossing, a section of Beverly, Massachusetts, he and his third wife, Nackey, called their residence in Nevada their legal home.

Since Nevada has no state income tax, the Loebs were no doubt pleased with the decision by Bay State tax officials in 1974 that their claim that Nevada was their primary residence was valid. But in 1980 that position was reversed, and nine days prior to his death in 1981 Loeb reached an interim settlement and paid the Bay State $314,000 in taxes "under protest."

Over the decades there have been countless newspaper and magazine articles on William Loeb. Often overlooked in what shaped and formed his life is the influence the West had on his views and outlook.

One of Loeb's daughters, Edith Tomasko, lives in the Granite State, something her father never managed to do. Asked whether he was more comfortable out west than in the east, she responded,

I think he was more comfortable there. It was an easy place for him to be. They had lots of friends there they visited every time they went out. Here I didn't see that. I saw there were political people and acquaintances and some friendships out of that but they were "let's get together because they're friends" type of thing. The West afforded him to—the expression is "let your hair down" but he didn't have any—but it allowed him to relax and not have to be Bill Loeb so much. I think here he felt he had to do that. Here we had to go to the opera because it was something you should do.

He was much more comfortable [out west]. He liked to ride and he liked to play tennis and he liked to ski and he really enjoyed doing it there. He liked the fact he could talk to anybody on the street and that's how it is out in the West, anybody talks to you; here you don't do that. Plus he had the whole reputation here to deal with.

In a letter to Hugh Gregg, Loeb wrote on Oct. 1, 1974,

I wish Nackey and I could show you this country out here. Right now it is magnificent. The temperature is up in the 80's during the day and down into the 30's at night; one sunny day follows another. I have been working mornings and getting up into the mountains on horseback every afternoon. We ride out of the back of our ranch, and it is unbelievably beautiful. Up at the top of the mountain we look down at Lake Tahoe on one side and the mountains of Nevada spreading away to the east. We practically never see anyone else on horseback.

Over the years a number of individuals from the Granite State made the trek down to William and Nackey Loeb's palatial mansion in Prides Crossing, Massachusetts. However, only a few traveled all the way out to Nevada to visit the couple at their legal residence. One such couple was William and Vivian Treat of Stratham. Married in 1947, two years later Bill Treat opened a law practice in the town of Hampton. He later became a banker, probate judge and a leader in the state GOP.

From 1954 to 1958 Treat served as chairman of the Republican State Committee and from 1960 to 1964 as Republican National Committeeman. He and his wife, who was also involved in many local and state activities, traveled a great deal, including to the West, where they would spend some time in the Sagebrush State with the Loebs.

In an interview on September 27, 2000, in Stratham, Bill Treat would find it difficult to contain his enthusiasm for that region of the country:

Anybody that goes to the West, particularly if you go into the back country of the West, immediately feels the difference, just in the physical environment.

I know that when we went riding there, as we did with the Loebs and others, and you're out in the vast open space and the sky looks about 10 times as big as it does in New

Hampshire and you just have this feeling—God—this is great. I just want to be left alone. I don't want to be bothered.

Nackey fitted into the saddle as if she were born to it. She was an expert horsewoman. Bill Loeb was like I was, more or less—he hung on for dear life, but Nackey belonged in the West, she grew up in the West, she obviously felt at home.

Speaking more about the attitude of the region that the Loebs adopted as their home, Treat observed,

It's a very obvious demographic distinction in this country. It's demonstrated in every election—California, New York, Massachusetts and so on are totally different than something like Utah, Wyoming and Montana. And a lot of it has to do with, I think, the style of life that is created, eventually that is created by virtue of where you live.

The former GOP leader, who was often suggested for but never sought the governorship of his adopted state (he was born in Boston and raised in Winterport, Maine) added, "Many of my friends here in the East when they want to go on vacation they *turn* east—they go to Europe, they go to London, they go to Paris, they go to Rome. A lot of them have never *been* to the West—particularly have never seen Yosemite or Jackson Hole, which to my mind is the most beautiful part of the country."

In presidential matches the *Union Leader* has seen the individuals it's given its editorial blessing win just three times in GOP primaries.

The first was in 1968, when it supported former vice president Richard Nixon. It came up a winner again with former California governor Ronald Reagan in 1980. It also appeared in the winner's circle embracing commentator Pat Buchanan in 1996.

The election of Ronald Reagan to the presidency was surely

the crowning glory of Bill Loeb's conservative political agenda. Loeb's daughter Edith said about the Reagan–Loeb connection: "He really liked Ronald Reagan a lot. Part of it, I think, was Ronald Reagan had a hero quality about him and part of it was his film stuff, and you know—it's an old western thing."

Leaving aside the noncompetitive GOP races in 1956, 1960 and 1984, this means that in 1952 (Ike over Taft), in 1964 (the write-in for Henry Cabot Lodge over Barry Goldwater), in 1972 (Nixon over John Ashbrook), in 1976 (Ford over Reagan), in 1988 (George H. W. Bush against Pierre du Pont IV), in 1992 (Bush against Bob Dole) and 2000 (McCain over Steve Forbes)—seven times the *Union Leader* has embraced candidates rejected by the GOP electorate.

Rarely asked in the reams of reporting and analysis regarding the power and influence over the first primary state that this newspaper and its sister publication, the *New Hampshire Sunday News* has, is whether the paper is really influential, or whether it simply fills a vacuum left by the eight other daily newspapers around the state.

In an interview with Eric Veblen, author of *The Manchester Union Leader in New Hampshire Elections*, published in 1975 by the University Press, William Johnson, an unsuccessful GOP U.S. Senate aspirant in 1966, stated,

> as to what he told the non-*Union Leader* editors: "You know, you people are the kind of guys who think that when you endorse a politician on Thursday prior to the election on Tuesday—that's that—you've really done him a great favor. What you don't recognize is in the meantime that Bill Loeb will be endorsing his opponent. But he doesn't do it once; he does it fourteen, fifteen, eighteen, twenty times, on page one. In the meantime he kicks your candidate in the fanny ten times by saying what an S.O.B. he is."

It does seem that the rest of the state's daily press has a self-imposed nonaggression pact when it comes to a policy of vigorous reporting on campaigns, leaving the Manchester daily in position to set the agenda.

Since that statement by Bill Johnson, there still has not been a more vigorous advocacy for candidates whom the non-*Union Leader* press has decided to support. In fact the opposite has taken place; the Manchester paper is nowhere near the strident organ it was in William Loeb's heyday.

As an example, it took until Aug. 8, 2002, for the paper to endorse Gordon Humphrey for governor, just 34 days before the Sept. 10 state primary decision. The page one editorial written by publisher Joseph McQuaid said in part,

> Humphrey is also the strongest hope Republican conservatives have of stopping billionaire Craig Benson from buying his way to the nomination. Having unlimited money is nice but it cannot mask an untested, undefined political philosophy. It would be a shame for New Hampshire to go down that big-money-buys-all road. Fortunately, Gordon Humphrey is there to stop it.

And it wasn't until Aug. 25, just 17 days before the same state primary, this time for the U.S. Senate nomination, that the paper blessed in another McQuaid front-page editorial (this time in the *New Hampshire Sunday News*) First District U.S. representative John E. Sununu over two-term incumbent senator Bob Smith.

That editorial in part noted,

> If incumbent Bob Smith were still anything like the spunky, fight-for-the-little-guy this newspaper eagerly endorsed in the past, this might be a tougher call. But Mr. Smith has gone from Mr. Outsider to Mr. Insider, proudly boasting that his "seniority," his fundraising, and his ability to spend taxpayers' money are reason enough to keep him still longer in Washington after almost 20 years there.

There are better reasons to pick someone to represent our state.

According to the *Gale Directory of Publications and Broadcast Media*, the Manchester newspapers continue to dwarf all other papers in the state in terms of circulation. the *Union Leader* has a daily circulation of 62,000; the *Telegraph* is second with 26,890. The *New Hampshire Sunday News* leads in the weekly category with a circulation of 82,474; second is the *Sunday Telegraph* of Nashua with 33,183.

Loeb's background gives clues to his views and his and the *Leader*'s influence.

On Sept. 19, 1937, William Loeb's father died of pneumonia after an illness of a dozen days. Loeb, age 70, had since 1900 maintained a residence on West Shore Road, Oyster Bay, New York, near the Sagamore Hill home of Theodore Roosevelt.

Trained as a stenographer, he began work for Roosevelt in 1899 during Roosevelt's first year as governor of the Empire State.

In his obituary in the *New York Times* it was noted of William Loeb II: "He was not only a secretary; he was a factotum, a go-between, a buffer between the impetuosity of an impulsive president and the equally impetuous office seekers. Gradually he became indispensable and a most important personage at the White House."

In the chapter of *The Invisible Presidency* that author Louis Koenig devoted to Loeb's father, he wrote,

In various ways, Loeb's personality was well attuned to the necessities of T.R. An actor who hogged the stage, the President didn't tolerate competition from his colleagues for public attention. With one or two exceptions, his cabinet was a pack of drab personalities utterly incapable of evoking a flicker of popular enthusiasm. Loeb's personality coloration, too, blended nicely with the necessity of his complete self-subordination as a condition of employment. Serving T.R. was the central event, the final ambition, the crowning achievement of William Loeb's life.

On the job and off, his style was unremittingly unobtrusive. Quiet, courteous and imperturbable, mild in humor and free from airs, his inner nature matched his outer self.

Koenig also noted: "Loeb was in all but name the President's press secretary. He was kept busy in his quasi-official capacity because T.R. was a genius in publicly dramatizing the issues of the day and in resourcefully inventing them when they were in short supply."

William Loeb III was born in Washington, D.C., on Dec. 26, 1905. At his christening his godparents were President and Mrs. Theodore Roosevelt. In a clear case of someone taking after his godfather and not his own father, the younger Loeb years later developed a Hearstian appetite for attention and notoriety.

Except for someone like T.R., it would be difficult for anyone to match William Loeb III and his ability to draw attention to himself and his publication. Loeb became a master at establishing the parameters for discussing public policy questions and at building up and tearing down political candidates and other public figures when the spirit moved him, as it so often did.

Few were able to match his instinct for the jugular, an instinct given plenty of exposure in his famous front-page editorials (by one count more than 6,000) scolding leaders or ideas opposed to his extremely conservative viewpoint.

Joseph McQuaid has worked for the paper all of his adult life. Since May 1999 he has been the president and publisher of the *Union Leader* and *New Hampshire Sunday News*, as well as the Union Leader Corp. When interviewed for the documentary on the life of William Loeb produced by John Gfroerer in 2001 and titled "Powerful as Truth," McQuaid said of his late boss: "His father was *de facto* White House chief of staff for Theodore Roosevelt, one of the cutting figures of the country. Loeb is Roosevelt's godson, born at the seat of power and I think wanted to be a player at the seat of power."

Another source wrote of the influence that T.R. had on Loeb III that he "not only exerted a close, constant influence on him through his formative years but remains his exemplar to this day."

Given all the controversy that swirled around his life (and his three marriages), William Loeb clearly could never have been a candidate for president. But if he couldn't be king, having control of the first primary state's most powerful media organ did permit him to become kingmaker.

A lengthy feature on Loeb in the Jan. 10, 1975, issue of the magazine *New Times* by Robert Sam Anson and Gordon Weil noted that "in 1949, at Loeb's urging, the state legislature voted to set the date of New Hampshire's presidential primary earlier than that of any other state in the nation."

William Gardner of Manchester has been the secretary of state for the Granite State since 1976 and he is obviously a leading authority on the history of the primary. Asked whether the observation by Anson and Weil was correct, he simply stated, "It didn't happen."

Starting in 1950 Loeb was willing to let everyone know he was quite willing to use the daily he had acquired for $1.25 million from Mrs. Frank Knox in November 1946 as his bully pulpit. His editorial blessing of Wesley Powell, a former chief of staff to one of his favorite politicians, Sen. Styles Bridges, set the standard for so many Granite State contests to follow for the next three decades.

In the Republican primary in September 1950, two-term senator Charles Tobey won renomination by just 1,310 votes over Powell, and in November he defeated North Country Democrat Emmet Kelley of Berlin by 33,669 votes.

In election after election the tactics Loeb always used with varying degrees of success were to burnish the neo-conservative populist credentials of the candidates he had given his editorial blessing to and at the same time portray those in opposition as members in good standing of the economic and political elite.

A dozen years after the Tobey–Powell tussle some Republicans did some homework on the publisher and in a campaign flyer took aim at Loeb and his own populism—or lack thereof.

Three GOP state senators—Edward Bennett of Bristol, James Cleveland of New London and James Rogers of Laconia—produced a flyer that proclaimed at the bottom: "We are Republican State Senators who live in New Hampshire, vote in New Hampshire, pay taxes in New Hampshire and register our cars in New Hampshire." At the top of the flyer was an aerial photograph of "(The residence of William Loeb, Pride's Crossing, Mass., with main house located on 43 acres of land, two small houses (servants' quarters), a big swimming pool, a greenhouse, a garage and a storehouse.)" The question was posed: "IS THIS THE CAPITAL OF NEW HAMPSHIRE?"

Obviously the publisher had gotten under the skin of these officeholders as they leveled the charge of carpetbagger:

> It is the palatial residence of William Loeb, publisher of the Manchester Union-Leader. Loeb lives in this palace in Massachusetts. He does not live in New Hampshire, vote in New Hampshire, pay personal taxes in New Hampshire or even register his cars in New Hampshire, not even his $8,000 sports car.
>
> From this palace at Prides Crossing, Loeb directs his puppets who are trying to seize political power in New Hampshire. It is time the citizens of New Hampshire repudiated this man and his palace guard, the puppets of Prides Crossing.

In an effort to clear up any confusion it also exhorted, "Let's keep the capital of New Hampshire in New Hampshire."

New Hampshire historian Stuart Wallace noted in the documentary on Loeb: "The real power among conservative Republicans anyway was Styles Bridges and he always recognized that when Bridges was alive. Bridges and Loeb get along fairly well because they can help each other. But he always recognized that Bridges was the leader of the conservative Republicans."

Recalling what took place in the wild election year of 1962 in the race to fill the remaining four years for the Bridges seat and decide whether Governor Wesley Powell could win a third consecutive two-year term (something that had not occurred in the state yet), Wallace noted,

> The impact of Loeb and the *Union Leader* is greatest in the primaries—particularly in the Republican primary. And the problem was that is we have a long primary season where you have a lot of time to open up wounds—and nobody could open up wounds any better than William Loeb. Then you only have a couple of months to sort of lick those wounds. In 1962 there was no wound licking going on. Powell turned around and backed John King.

Although the abysmal track record in blessing candidates in the presidential primary is quite obvious, the actual amount of influence the paper wields has always been a matter of dispute. In their 1975 article in *New Times*, authors Anson and Weil mentioned that "even Loeb's enemies concede that an endorsement from the *Union Leader* means an automatic 15 to 20 percent of the vote."

That statement is all the more remarkable given the fact that in the primary (1972) just before the article was published, the only Democrat ever to receive the full Loeb-press laying-on-of-hands, Los Angeles mayor Samuel Yorty, reaped just 5,401 supporters at the polls, finishing behind senators Muskie and McGovern with just 6% of the vote.

In his book on the newspaper Eric Veblen wrote,

> Loeb set out to make Yorty a household word as soon as
> he announced his candidacy on November 16, 1971. From the
> day after the news of Yorty's announcement (November 18)
> until primary election day (March 7), the *Leader*'s "sample
> pages" carried 71 stories and 30 photographs of Yorty, along
> with 14 editorials supporting him. Some of the coverage
> apparently was designed to appeal to Manchester's Irish and
> Franco-American voters—such as a story and photo about
> Yorty visiting his mother's home village in Ireland, and a
> photo of Yorty receiving the award of Knight of the Legion of
> Honor from French Prime Minister Jacques Chaban-Delmas.

In his 1996 autobiography *Combat*, former senator Warren
Rudman wrote of Loeb: "People often asked me what made Bill
Loeb tick, but I never knew the answer. There must have been
some great anger or frustration that drove him to use his power in
such mean-spirited ways."

Asked her response to this quotation, Loeb's daughter Edith
said, "I don't think he was mean-spirited. I think he just did what
he felt was right. Sometimes it wasn't that pleasant and sometimes
he really walked over people and crushed them."

Michael Birkner has taught at Gettysburg College since 1989
and has been chairman of the history department since 1993 and a
full professor since 1995. In an interview conducted in Concord on
July 26, 2002, as to what the legacy of William Loeb is, Birkner
answered,

> I think he made it very difficult for the state to have [what]
> as an outsider I would call a responsible approach to tax policy.
> I think that Loeb tended to hit anybody over the head with a
> two-by-four or worse who even suggested that a broad-based
> tax could be a possible answer to specific ways that the state

was falling short in services. I think that was a problem as a legacy while he was alive and it was left to the next generation—and we still haven't come out from under that.

Birkner has been researching a biography on Sherman Adams for a number of years. In elaborating on the Loeb legacy, he added: "If you have a picture of the New England states New Hampshire is the one that doesn't quite fit the pattern. That's also true in terms of partisan alignment right now." He noted that New England and the Pacific Coast are the most Democratic regions in the nation, but New Hampshire is the exception in New England. He stated: "The *Union Leader* doesn't have the fangs it used to have, it doesn't have the clout it used to have."

As for her opinion of the changing world newspapers have to deal with, Loeb's daughter Edith said, "Today papers need to survive by also giving people different viewpoints and allowing readers to choose more so. My dad never would have done this. He just wouldn't have done it."

The confrontation between the *Leader* and Edmund Muskie was a significant example of Loeb's tactics and influence.

In an interview in Topsham, Maine, on April 7, 1979, John Cole, the founding editor of the *Maine Times* (who died on Jan. 8, 2003), said of Senator Muskie,

> Muskie was following a predescribed course. He and others rebuilt the Democratic Party here in Maine. They made it into a two-party state. But at the top the pressures would become much greater. That's when you become exposed as it were—every weakness is there—under that kind of pressure.
>
> People close to Muskie and who knew him all those years knew he had those weaknesses. He's stubborn, he likes to argue, he had a good mind, but he doesn't have the fire—

you've got to have the force—you've got to have that drive. Look at Ed Muskie today and you can understand why he didn't make it. Now it happens to all of us, now he doesn't have any drive at all. He lacked that extra thing and when you get right down to it—it's that extra sort of drive—I don't know what else to call it—that gets people to the presidency.

Left unsaid in this comment is that Ed Muskie had a temper. There was a time when presidential candidates were nominated in smoke-filled rooms and conventions and just a miniscule group of party leaders decided who would be awarded the presidential nomination. Having a temper (à la Harry Truman) wasn't always a handicap.

Matters have undergone quite a change with party leaders having lost considerable influence to the voters in the stress-filled and exhausting primaries (40 in 2000). With the electorate in turn having to share their power with the media, the only effective way to reach the millions of voters who participate is via television, the Internet, newspaper, radio and magazine exposure.

There are those who believe that the media have shortcomings in vetting the presidential field. Back in 1983 when Ohio Democratic senator John Glenn was a bright and shining star, many who had a chance to hear him in person were left cold.

The media determined that the Democratic race would be between frontrunner former vice president Walter Mondale and Glenn. In the end this equation was to be only half-right.

It might have helped Glenn if in running in the 1984 primary here he'd been able to turn to a major Democratic officeholder for assistance, but none was in his corner then. Every major office save one was in the hands of the GOP, so Glenn, with no national campaign experience, was on his own—and it showed.

As Hubert Humphrey's running mate in 1968, Edmund Muskie had one national campaign under his belt, yet when it

comes time to do battle, for several reasons it helps to have someone nearby to act in some combination as a guide, mentor, sound-
ing board and troubleshooter.

During rough patches of a campaign it helps to have someone
available with the background, trust and respect to help overcome
the difficult times with not only one's dignity but also one's campaign intact.

While writing the book *First in the Nation*, I conducted two
interviews with Sen. Thomas McIntyre. In the second one, conducted in his office in the federal building in downtown
Manchester, the senator on Sept. 13, 1976, reflected on why he
wasn't able to help his beleaguered colleague from the neighboring state of Maine:

> The time he [Muskie] got in trouble up here, I was in
> trouble physically. As the result of a physical examination I
> had been told by mid-February that I faced *serious* surgery. It
> was for an abdominal aneurysm. I was very upset about it. I
> was due to enter Johns Hopkins on March 2, 1972. This oper-
> ation had been on my mind for two to three weeks.
>
> It was a time of great turmoil for me. I became very agi-
> tated. This is a serious operation. Eight, nine hours of surgery.
> It was a traumatic mental experience for me. I wasn't keeping
> tabs on things up here and I don't know if I'd been healthy
> and seen trouble coming I could have helped. I always
> thought somebody tried to have him do what John F. Kennedy
> [did] on election eve in 1960.

McIntyre was referring to the general election-eve speech in
1960 that Kennedy gave within shouting distance of the *Union Leader*
which Kennedy aide Ted Sorensen later wrote was "a rare show of
public irritability and incaution in blasting one local publisher for
saying once again that Kennedy was a Communist sympathizer."

Bill Dunfey, the coordinator for northern New England for the senator from the Bay State in the general election said,

> John Kennedy did the same thing and fell into the same trap that Ed Muskie did. Only he was lucky—it was the night before the election. Some of those who'd followed the nominee for months couldn't believe that somebody could get under his skin that much. He'd always had the ability to rise above the heat of the battle and not let things get the best of his emotion, but not this time.

The attack came so late that Loeb missed the opportunity to place one of his famed front-page rebuttals in the election day morning edition. He did manage to fire off some salvos in a news story: "Kennedy's tirade indicates Kennedy is lacking in the basic dignity expected of a president of the United States." He was called a "liar and a spoiled brat . . . his childish ranting last night shows that he is completely lacking in the necessary stature to be president of the United States."

On Feb. 24, 1972, regarding the "Canuck" reference Edmund Muskie had supposedly made in Florida 13 days before, Loeb wrote in one of his famous front-page signed editorials, "If Paul Morrison, the author of the letter, hadn't taken the trouble to write about his experience with Senator Muskie in Florida, no one in New Hampshire would know of the derogatory remarks emanating from the Muskie camp about the Franco-Americans in New Hampshire and Maine—remarks which the senator found amusing."

In his 1979 book *The Fear Brokers*, written with John Obert, Senator McIntyre reflected that "as Loeb's assaults on Muskie grew more and more vicious, I chafed to get into the primary fray, to go back home, stand by Ed Muskie, defend him and extol him, but I had given my word I would not."

The senator recounted the bitter primary in 1968 and how the wounds of the Johnson and McCarthy partisans had taken a long time to heal and "after that campaign I promised I would never again take an active role in a presidential primary. At the outset of the 1972 primary I announced that I would vote for Edmund Muskie but beyond that simple declaration would play no part in his campaign."

The author of the infamous letter from Florida has never been identified and what is often overlooked in much of the reporting of what transpired was the fact that "Ed Muskie's sisters are married to men of French descent," according to McIntyre's book.

Also receiving scant attention was the fact that during his single term as governor of the Pine Tree State, Muskie appointed more Franco-Americans to state government posts than any governor before him.

There is no denying the fact that Loeb influenced the decision that was made on March 7, 1972. As George Mitchell said during an interview at his home in Cape Elizabeth, Maine, on June 5, 1976,

> I think he certainly did have an influence in 1972. He obviously chose Muskie as his principal target, and left McGovern alone when given his history it would have been natural to assume that McGovern's views would have been the very antithesis of Loeb's views and not Muskie's . . . [Loeb] did have an adverse effect on Muskie's campaign.

Of the infamous letter from Florida even Joe McQuaid conceded in the program "Powerful as Truth" that the authorship of the Canuck letter had never been authentically proven. "But I would bet you dollars to doughnuts it wasn't any kid named Paul Morrison. I'm pretty convinced it was a dirty trick and I think Loeb got played for a willing sucker on that."

In defeating McGovern by 46% to 37%, Muskie carried seven of the 10 counties; however, populous Hillsborough County, which contains the two largest cities in the state—Manchester and Nashua—was Muskie's weakest winning county (43%). In addition, although the future secretary of state in the Carter administration won 11 of the 13 cities, the vote he reaped in Manchester—38%—was by far the poorest he tallied of all the cities he won. Muskie, a product of the northwestern Maine community of Rumford, received 70% in Somersworth, near the Maine border, and 65% in Berlin, a North Country mill city not far from his native Rumford.

The Loeb attack on Muskie was referred to by one Columbia University journalism professor as "the most sustained, gut-level attack directed toward any individual in modern history." Since that was written it is doubtful that anything has transpired in a presidential campaign that would contradict that statement.

Yet to lay all the blame for Muskie's failure to win the nomination at Loeb's door misses a body of evidence that shows that his failure as a candidate was a multifaceted phenomenon.

One has to factor in the ineptness, mismanagement and overconfidence of the campaign itself. Muskie lacked the drive and stamina to withstand the trials and tribulations along the primary and caucus trail and he failed to forcefully articulate his positions on the issues of the day, preferring to take his stand on the time-worn slogan of "Trust Muskie."

It also misses the substantial foul-ups brought about by the importation of many out-of-state organizers whose actions forced one Cheshire County Democrat to send this lament to the state headquarters in Manchester: "No campaign has ever been run with so little regard for the local organization and, as a result, people involved at the local level are becoming frustrated, confused, discouraged and distrusting. Further, we are faced with having in January a group that will dissolve itself before March."

Neal Peirce served as a consultant for CBS News in 1962 as well as from 1967 to 1976. He worked in a similar capacity for NBC News from 1964 to 1966. With such an extensive background in researching and writing about America, he understands the political leadership in this nation as well as anyone.

He was asked, since a president of the United States has to deal with other leaders who are far more difficult to negotiate with than William Loeb ever was, if Muskie couldn't handle Loeb and his attacks, did he have the temperament to be president?

Peirce answered,

> Well, there was an emotional side to Muskie—it was well documented and people wrote about it and I actually referred to it in my book as I recall [see Chapter 1, this volume].
>
> On the other hand I think he was one of the great public figures of his time and a man of splendid breadth and depth, so I'm not sure that the fact that you can become very emotional about an attack on your wife is a satisfactory measure of what your performance would be under the pressures of the presidency.
>
> It's conceivable but it's not a case that I would automatically make. Especially given the long-term good judgment and intelligence of the individual involved here and his breadth of views as to this state, his community, what America stood for, our role in the world, he was [a] class A public servant.
>
> Muskie does, of course, have character traits problematic for a presidential candidate. One is his frequent aloofness, another his towering temper, and still another his insistence on learning all sides of an issue, mulling it over carefully in his mind, before taking a stand. Finally, he lacks the burning ambition, the steely determination that has sustained men like Humphrey, Nixon, and McGovern in campaigns for the presidency, even when the odds seemed hopelessly against them.

On Muskie's appearance on a snowy Saturday morning, Feb. 26, in front of the Union Leader building, I recall being briefly told about what had transpired in Manchester by Field Reichardt, state deputy campaign manager for Pete McCloskey, in the Concord headquarters in the late afternoon.

I made a point of watching the "CBS Evening News" that Saturday and the contempt I felt for someone like Loeb was about as great as I'd felt for another human being.

However, as the saying goes, upon further review I wish that more people had had a chance to watch the film of what happened that day beyond the brief close-up clip of the senator from Maine choking up on the makeshift platform—the trailer of a flatbed truck.

Researching the documentary on William Loeb and looking at some additional footage gives one a better understanding of just how fierce the snowstorm was, thereby making the call on whether Senator Muskie shed real tears all the more impossible.

This event has already been covered in detail, as well in my book *First in the Nation*. Yet it still stands to many as the defining moment of the primary history, and also as the point at which reporters and others turned (at least for a time) against the first vote as something of value to this nation's political process.

As despicable as William Loeb often was, it was still a test to see how a presidential contender and his advisers managed to handle the venom that Loeb could generate. If you could take it, clearly you had passed one important test to prove you were ready for the presidency, and if you failed, as Muskie clearly did, you were not.

As the presidential bandwagon of Edmund Sixtus Muskie rolled into the state capital of Concord on a cold Jan. 6, 1972, a couple of us in the McCloskey for President headquarters across from the capitol building weren't pleased. Situated in a storefront on the ground floor of the historic Eagle Hotel (at that time a nursing home and later to become an office building), another McCloskey staffer, Eric Schnapper, and I discussed how to make a statement of just what we thought of Muskie's arrival.

Schnapper, from New York City and a recent graduate of Yale Law School, had performed the same role as advance man in Eugene McCarthy's bid here four years earlier; the two of us finally settled on just what would be done.

One of us, I honestly don't remember who, came up with the idea of donating some Styrofoam cups, since on such a frigid day coffee would be a hot commodity.

I was all set to find some McCloskey stickers to affix to the bottom of the cups when Schnapper, the wily vet of a previous presidential primary and someone who clearly had achieved a far higher degree of duplicitous behavior, suggested that we place McGovern stickers on the bottoms of the cups instead.

Once that was done I walked across the street to the State House plaza, past a statue of the 14th president of the United States, Franklin Pierce, the only Granite Stater ever to win election to the Oval Office.

Standing behind a table and near a statue of Daniel Webster was Maria Carrier, then of Manchester and now of Washington, D.C. A McCarthy delegate to the national convention in 1968, she was the state coordinator for, as he was referred to, "the man from Maine."

Carrier, a rather charming person, thanked me for the coffee cups and that was the last I ever expected to hear about the matter. It was just a prank, something from the Dick Tuck School of Campaign Hijinks. Tuck, for those too young to have heard about him, for years managed to rattle Republicans (especially Richard Nixon) with zany ideas to try to break their campaign rhythm.

In *Breach of Faith—the Fall of Richard Nixon*, published in 1975, after mentioning the dirty tricks operation organized by the Nixon White House in 1972, author Theodore White wrote of Tuck,

Dirty tricks are as old as American campaigning, as old, indeed, as electoral politics, dating back to republican Rome. But they had been elevated to a minor dark art by another graduate of a Southern California university, the celebrated Democratic prankster Dick Tuck, a political wit who had specialized for twelve years in plaguing and pin-pricking Richard Nixon's campaigns.

One has to keep in mind that since this was 1972, the year the all-out assault by the Committee to Re-elect the President (CREEP) was launched on behalf of Richard Nixon and unleashed against Senator Muskie to make sure the man regarded as the most serious challenger to a second term for Nixon was derailed. And derailed he was, yet the bag of Republican dirty tricks continued, witness the break-in to the headquarters of the Democratic National Committee on June 27, 1972, which eventually led to Nixon's resignation on Aug. 9, 1974.

The Nixon team wasn't as concerned about McCloskey as they were Muskie, but I do recall briefly talking with Tony Ulasewicz after McCloskey spoke at Dartmouth. The retired New York City detective was not a newspaper reporter from New York City as he represented himself, but someone hired as the White House private eye to keep tabs on the McCloskey operation, along with other chores. He later became infamous when it was revealed that he was a bag man who delivered sizable sums of money to those caught in the web of crime and deceit as the Watergate scandal unfolded.

In the book *They Could Not Trust the King*, published in 1974 by Collier Books, author William V. Shannon wrote,

Tony Ulasewicz, the paunchy, jowly retired detective who served as Kalmbach's agent in the delivery of money to the Watergate burglars, provided the hearings with their only sustained comic relief. With vivid colloquialisms, deadpan delivery, and the street-wise attitudes of an old cop who has spent his professional life on intimate terms with sin, Ulasewicz seemed to have stepped into the Caucus Room out of the pages of Damon Runyon.

After that campaign, by the summer of 1973 I was living in a log cabin I'd helped to construct in the town of Sutton, near Lake Sunapee, and was working as a winder in a woolen mill in the town of Newport.

Without any electricity and certainly with no TV I managed to miss the Watergate hearings that transfixed so much of the country in the summer and fall of '73.

By the time I'd moved back to Concord in the fall I was taken aback, while visiting some friends in the town of Dunbarton, to hear Art and Fran Gewehr describe some of the testimony of that day's hearing.

That day the political director for the McGovern campaign, Frank Mankiewicz, testified before the Select Committee on Presidential Campaign Activities of the United States Senate, concerning Watergate and related activities. He appeared on Thursday afternoon, Oct. 13, 1973.

Questioned primarily by Samuel Dash, chief counsel and staff director for the select committee, Mankiewicz appeared without counsel. This aide to Senator McGovern, who also worked for Sen. Robert Kennedy from 1966 until his death in June 1968, delivered an opening statement that said in part,

> I think it is important for someone to state, clearly and firmly, that these "dirty tricks" are not politics as usual—that American politics does not include any history of, or tolerance for sabotage, espionage, perjury, forgery or burglary. The political process does not, and has not, countenanced firebombing of Government institutions or the slandering of an opponent by accusing him of sexual misconduct—or, to be sure, slandering the memory of a slain President by the use of a forgery which accuses him of murder. . . . And it has certainly never included—at the Presidential level—using agencies of Government to harass and punish your "enemies" nor the use

of special White House gumshoes to count the bottles in a Senator's trash.

He added that the "dirty tricks" that were the legacy of the just concluded 1972 presidential election managed to "create within the Democratic Party such a strong sense of resentment among the candidates and their followers as to make unity of the party impossible once a nominee was selected. At that, the effort seems to have been most successful."

Mankiewicz is a graduate of UCLA, class of '47, which also included H. R. Haldeman and John Ehrlichman, the two top aides to President Nixon who served time for their Watergate-related activities.

As his testimony progressed he dealt with how the McGovern campaign tried to deal with the disruptions the Nixon team was able to create, problems that heightened the infighting among the Democratic campaigns of Muskie, McGovern and Humphrey.

About halfway through his testimony the McGovern political director was asked by attorney Dash if he knew Dick Tuck. "I know him very well" was the answer. He said that his guess was he'd first gotten to know him in the 1960 campaign in California, where Mankiewicz was practicing law and active in Democratic Party politics. He also worked with Tuck in RFK's 1968 campaign and "I was responsible for his being hired in the 1972 campaign, and in the interim I see him from time to time, and I would say we are friends as well as associates."

He then described what happened the day Senator Muskie ventured to the Granite State to file his candidacy in the primary:

> In New Hampshire when any candidate files for the Presidential primary, the Governor sponsors a sort of coffee-and-cake reception in the statehouse after the candidate has filed his papers, and when Senator Muskie went up there in

January 1972 they had this reception, and as the guests finished their coffee, they all discovered that underneath the coffee as they turned up their cups, pasted on the bottom looking up at you, was a replica of a McGovern campaign button. Now, that doesn't get into the league of some of the things we have been talking about here. But it is in my view toward the bottom range of a Dick Tuck–type operation, and as a matter of fact, I called Dick that afternoon to congratulate him on it, and he said no, he hadn't done it, but I assume it was done by a disciple.

Shortly after I confessed my role in the coffee cup caper to the Gewehrs, I was speaking to a friend and told her I was thinking of writing a first-person confession of my role in this incident for the weekly *New Hampshire Times*, a publication I'd done some freelance writing for. This friend felt such a confession would hurt my political future—and I decided not to write about it—until now.

Muskie's and the *Leader*'s battle over the "Canuck" letter raises the issue of the significant Franco-American minority and their part in the political process in New Hampshire.

Manchester was incorporated as a town in 1751 and was first known as Derryfield. In 1810 the town's name was changed to Manchester, after the cotton mill center in England. It became the state's first city in 1846. In 1831 the state legislature approved the incorporation of the Amoskeag Manufacturing Company, a firm which became the dominant economic force in the city for a century.

At the midpoint of the 19th century, Amoskeag Manufacturing commenced the production of locomotives and during the 1850s manufactured 232 railroad engines. By 1860 the corporation began the production of steam fire engines; in the following 17 years 550 such engines were made. The company was situated on the banks of the Merrimack River in a massive collection of buildings. These structures, many of which are still standing, were made primarily of brick. The bricks were produced at the brickyards in Hooksett and then were floated down the river on barges.

In the last century one of the state's most notable historians was J. Duane Squires, a professor of history at Colby-Sawyer College in the toney community of New London, about halfway between the state capital of Concord and the town of Hanover, where Dartmouth College is located.

Squires wrote in his four-volume history, *The Granite State of the United States*, published in 1956,

> In its great days in the middle of the 19th century and thereafter for some decades, the Amoskeag Manufacturing Company was the largest cotton textile plant in the world. Its mills employed more than 15,000 persons. There were 650,000 cotton spindles, 78,000 worsted spindles, and 24,000 looms. Utilizing upward of 50 million pounds of cotton a year, the mills turned out cloth at the rate of more than a mile every minute of the working day. Their weekly payroll provided the livelihood for Manchester people, and they paid at least a third of all the city taxes.

The company managed to prosper during World War I, but in 1921 the management of Amoskeag announced a three-day work schedule and a 22.5% reduction in pay. The 16,000 textile workers accepted the cutbacks. By taking this step they hoped any further reductions could be prevented. The payroll of the company was about half the payroll of the city.

Within a year another reduction in pay was proclaimed, along with an increase in the work week. A vote of the unions presented in the mills showed that 12,032 employees were opposed to the wage reduction and only 188 were willing to accept it. Soon a long and bitter strike was on, and it lasted nine months. This struggle forced the company to accumulate losses from which it would not recover.

In the year 1932 Amoskeag lost more than $1 million and the following year there was another strike. According to Squires's history, this strike

> caused such unrest that Mayor Damase Caron requested military guards for the mill properties. The growing threat of southern mill competition was ever more ominous. There were continual "lay-offs" of the workers, and in 1933 and 1934 there was much unemployment and real privation in Manchester. The rumor grew that basic conditions in the big mills were bad. These rumors, unfortunately, were correct.

By late 1935 the company filed for bankruptcy, and in the following year a disastrous flood caused heavy damage to the mills and their equipment. By the fall of 1936 liquidation of the company was under way. At the time of the demise of Amoskeag Manufacturing a dedicated group of Manchester citizens created Amoskeag Industries Inc., a development group that bought all the properties except for an electric plant, which the Public Service Company of New Hampshire purchased for $2.5 million.

Manchester is located in Hillsborough County and is the county seat. It has a population of 107,000 residents, the state's largest, with 20,400 more people than Nashua, the second largest city.

Lacking the robust population growth in so many other cities and towns in the populous southern tier, Manchester's delegation to the state House of Representatives has shrunk from the 54 seats awarded after the 1950 census to just 35 after the 2000 one.

In 1961 the Joint Center for Urban Studies of MIT and Harvard University issued "A Report on Politics in Manchester, New Hampshire." The author, Robert Binstock, wrote in part,

> The development of a large, homogeneous French-Canadian community in Manchester, numbering today about

50,000, was linked to growth of the Amoskeag textile mills in the 19th century. From around 1837 to the end of the century, many large families migrated to Manchester from impoverished and over-populated farm lands in Quebec. They were among many discontented settlers in French-Canada who were attracted by industrial wages in nearby New England. By 1890, 70 percent of the French-Canadians in the United States were located in New England and 40 percent of all textile workers in New Hampshire were Canadian-born. This migration was sharply reduced by the return of economic prosperity to Quebec in 1900.

However, arrival in this nation did not necessarily mean assimilation. Binstock stated,

> In many ways the French-Canadian community forms a separate society in Manchester with institutions distinct from and parallel to those of its English-speaking neighbors. The French and the rest of the community sense a significant degree of mutual isolation. Basic to the French-Canadian culture is the concept of *la survivance*—a desire to retain the heritage of *les habitants,* to resist assimilation and loss of identity. *La survivance* has been continually emphasized in French-Canadian literature. The press has often urged its readers to speak French in the church, at home, in clubs and societies . . .

On the required reading list of every journalist who traipses up to cover the quadrennial electoral tribal rite should be the 1947 book *Inside U.S.A.,* by renowned roving reporter John Gunther.

Gunther, who died in May 1970, achieved celebrity status with his *Inside* books on Europe, Asia and Latin America. He began his career as a reporter with the *Chicago Daily News,* in the city where he was born in 1901.

His report on the Granite State contains the kind of texture and eye for nuance and detail that only a master of the writing craft can achieve. Just four of the 52 chapters in the book are devoted to New England, but the reader learns that the author believes that "New Hampshire—Massachusetts and New York aside—has probably contributed more men to American public life than any other eastern state."

In addition, Gunther—unlike so many of the writers about this state, does not hesitate to pull the varnish off public life: "Good Yankees describe urban labor as 'all that slum stuff' and I heard more anti-Semitic talk in New Hampshire than anywhere else in New England. Dartmouth, in the summer of 1945, got into a noisy peck of trouble because it was applying the quota system to limit attendance by Jewish students."

The author also put on his architectural critic's cap when he noted, "Concord, New Hampshire, has the ugliest state capitol I ever saw." He then listed the buildings around the central square including the State Library "with an amazingly hideous bell tower" which was torn down during the administration of Democratic Governor John King. Another building he listed was "an atrocity of a barn."

Gunther wrote of the French Canadians,

Probably this unique minority group, almost unknown to the nation at large, is the most tenacious in the entire country. There are 908,386 French Canadians in the United States, of whom the great majority are Roman Catholic; and almost all clustered in New England. Most of them came to the United States for the same reason that the Irish did—they were hungry, they needed jobs. And (I mean no offense) they represented communities in Quebec which for two hundred years had had extremely little opportunity for social or intellectual development. Look at parts of Quebec itself today. The French

Canadians now in this country almost never intermix; they hold with the utmost stubbornness and obstinacy to their own folklore, customs, language. A good many are farmers, some are urban dwellers; almost all vote Democratic, and they are a considerable source of power to the political machines in Maine and New Hampshire towns.

Certainly in the past half-century the Franco-American community in New Hampshire's largest city and other locales has become more assimilated. The key factor for this is the reality that since the 1960s English (rather than French) has become the primary language taught in the parochial schools. With this enhanced language ability students have been more capable of succeeding at secondary educational challenges in this region.

William Gardner, the state's secretary of state, was born and raised in the Queen City. He was elected to serve in the state legislature in both 1972 and 1974. Gardner recalled,

> If you look in the Redbook [the official record of election returns] if you look at the West Side in the '50s, '60s and '70s and you look at the names of those elected state representatives, they're all French names in the French wards. Now you don't see that. It's not like that much anymore. You might see one name in French, one name in English or Irish or Greek. That has changed over the last quarter century; there's less identity of an ethnic group.

In discussing the changing political picture in the Queen City, Martin Gross mentioned,

> Franco ethnicity or Irish ethnicity doesn't seem to count for much anymore in Democratic politics in Manchester. . . . [Manchester] was very tribal; it continues to be tribal—perhaps

not in the sense of traditional ethnicity but in a variety of other ways. There are people self-selecting the tribe; if you are not of their self-selected tribe you are the enemy. Or if someone has a grudge for you or a grudge for somebody, that seems to count more than anything else over a long period of time. . . .

I think the old power centers—which I would count to three—French, Irish and Labor—have declined in their power in Manchester. They don't tell the tale anymore. Neither the labor unions, nor the bishop, nor whoever else who used to tell people how to vote count much anymore. That's how Manchester has changed. I think the power of the *Manchester Union Leader* has declined somewhat in Manchester but it still is the only rag and what the *Union Leader* says probably counts for a lot in Manchester, just as what the *Concord Monitor* says editorially counts for quite a bit in Concord.

Anyone upset by the reference to the *Union Leader* as a "rag," should keep in mind that the appendix to Kevin Cash's *Who the Hell Is William Loeb*, published in 1975, contains in just over six pages "[a] glossary of some of the names, terms and phrases which have appeared in William Loeb's newspapers to describe public figures and institutions."

Gardner recounted,

When I was in my early elementary school years over half the schools in Manchester were Catholic schools—and about half of those Catholic schools were dual-language schools. All morning classes would be taught in French and in the afternoon the classes would be taught in English.

So the students grew up going to school learning both languages and being taught in both languages. That started to decline in the early 1960s.

The enrollment in Catholic schools of primary and secondary students reached a peak of 30,230 in 1964.

Gardner added, "As the new generation came along there's less of a memory of where they came from and they are more Americanized. . . . Without the schools they're losing the language. You don't have anybody under 40 in Manchester speaking French anymore."

Every decade or two there seems to be an election that proves to be a defining event in the history of the state, a historical pivot point, if you will. One such election was in 1934. The speculation and rumors that have swirled around the contest for governor, between Republican Styles Bridges and Democrat and Manchester native John L. Sullivan, are intriguing and troubling, all the more interesting for how little has been written about the election. Also, if one were to search for a precedent for what happened to Edmund Muskie in Manchester in the winter of 1972, the 1934 election would be the one to examine.

J. Duane Squires writes only briefly of this contest for governor, and he provides no review of the controversy it generated.

Similarly, the 1934 election is not mentioned in the Binstock study, and in the recent biography of Sen. Styles Bridges published in 2001 and written by James Kiepper, there is just a single paragraph regarding what transpired.

Yet one author was willing to wade into what was surely an ethnic morass and proffer a judgment: John Henry Bartlett of Portsmouth, who served as GOP governor from 1919 to 1921 and later wrote a number of books. Among his contributions to the history of his native state, Bartlett penned *A Synoptic History of the Granite State*, published in 1939.

Bartlett does not avoid the controversy of '34. He wrote,

At the election the vote resulted as follows: Bridges

89,481; Sullivan 87,019 or a meager plurality for Bridges of 2,462. A last-minute racial canard, a false publication circulated in Manchester among French-Americans was thought to have defeated Sullivan who was a World-War veteran, popular and one of the ablest lawyers in the state.

The most significant treatment of what transpired in the Queen City in the run-up to the vote was written by William Dunfey in his "A Short History of the Democratic Party in New Hampshire," a master's thesis submitted to the Department of Government at the University of New Hampshire in June 1954.

Although this was Bridges's initial run for political office, the closeness of the vote, the question as to what role his campaign may have played in exploiting ethnic tensions in Manchester, plus the power he began to accumulate as he quickly moved on to the U.S. Senate just two years afterward, all helped to make '34 a significant election.

The Democratic ticket that year was considered to be a balanced and strong one, led by Dartmouth graduate (class of '21) John Lawrence Sullivan, who had the drive to campaign in rural areas and not just in Manchester, always a sign of potential trouble for the dominant GOP.

The week before the vote in November 1934 was a rather hectic one: One issue was what to do about the Notre Dame bridge that had been damaged in a flood. Residents of the primarily West Side of the Queen City weren't enamored with the idea of having to use another span about a mile down the Merrimack.

According to Dunfey's thesis, "Thomas Jennings, an alderman from Ward Eleven in Manchester, was asked what was going to be done about the bridge. Jestingly he replied, 'Let the "Frogs" swim across.' Despite the fact that the remark was made in good humor, it caused a ripple of resentment, although Jennings was only a minor figure in the political picture."

As the election neared, the Democrats' expectations rose that as long as they could maintain their normal strength in the state's largest city, Sullivan and not Bridges would be the next governor.

A rally was then held in the center of the West Side with Sullivan as the main speaker. Dunfey wrote,

> Sullivan was able to speak French reasonably well. In an effort to establish rapport with the French audience, he delivered his speech in his best schoolbook French. Immediately following Sullivan's talk, Chairman [of the meeting] Fortin was on his feet and speaking with some vehemence in his native tongue. He denounced Sullivan for his "jargon-like" delivery. Fortin said that Sullivan had insulted the audience by not speaking in English, which the audience was able to understand. He stated that French was not Sullivan's native tongue and that Sullivan should not try to win the West Side with such a maneuver. Fortin's hostility to Sullivan made it clear that a serious French-Irish breach was in the making.

Dunfey then acknowledges that what occurred next was somewhat murky, but he concluded,

> The statement with reference to the bridge problem, "Let the 'Frogs' swim across the river," was circulated as *Sullivan*'s reply about the situation. This inflammatory remark attributed to Sullivan spread rapidly through the heavily populated French section once it had been started. Indignation and hostility towards the Irish candidate, Sullivan, was too strong to be counteracted. For those responsible for the plot, the timing had been almost perfect. Election day was at hand and the unfortunate Sullivan suffered heavily on the West Side, with Ward Twelve and Ward Thirteen the most obvious examples.

In the solitary biography on Bridges (*Styles Bridges: Yankee Senator*), published in 2001, James Kiepper wrote about the controversial election held on Nov. 6, 1934: "Bridges defeated Sullivan by only 2,462 votes, and he garnered more votes in Manchester's French-speaking wards than any other Republican on the state ticket. Even twenty-five years later, according to John Warrington, the quotation quickly brought a twinkle to Bridges' eye and an unconvincing denial to his lips." (Warrington was Bridges's last administrative assistant and the derogatory reference was different from the one in the Dunfey thesis: "Let the frogs hop across the lily pads.")

After this razor-thin triumph and following the two-year term as governor, Bridges won election to the U.S. Senate by 8,728 votes. From that point on Bridges won reelection by increasing margins and his final victory was in 1960 with 60.3% of the vote. On November 26, 1961, he succumbed to a heart attack at his East Concord residence, which is now the official (albeit rarely used) residence of the governor.

There has never been a survey conducted to determine who was the most powerful person in New Hampshire in the last century, or a survey to determine who the 10 most powerful were. It is my contention that allies Bridges and Loeb would likely show up on the lists of most of those asked to respond to such a survey. And these two men would be at the top of any list of an awful lot of those questioned. This is in spite of the fact that Loeb never did maintain a residence in this state.

Several decades ago a Democratic party leader stated, "Every Democratic primary in New Hampshire is an Irish versus French-Canadian struggle." That is no longer the case, but a remnant of gender and ethnic discrimination still does exist in this state, although it is rarely written about and discussed, at least not in public.

Binstock also wrote about this struggle:

Conflict between the French-Canadian and Irish of Manchester is more than a contest for political stature. It is the outgrowth of a deep-rooted historical enmity. Early Canadian émigrés to New England were often subjected to violence from Irish mill hands who resented the newcomers' acceptance of lower wages and their reluctance to strike. But a more enduring animosity was engendered by quarrels within the Catholic Church. Irish domination of the church hierarchy through the 19th century provoked widespread resentment among the French-Canadians.

It is, after all, a matter of record that no one of Franco-American heritage has ever been elected to statewide office. The only major office that someone of the largest ethnic group in this state has been able to carry is the First Congressional District seat; the last was Democrat Norman D'Amours of Manchester, who was elected to the first of five terms with the Watergate class of 1974. D'Amours gave up the seat in 1984 as he lost his bid for the U.S. Senate to first-term GOP senator Gordon Humphrey by 68,381 votes.

Furthermore, the New Hampshire Republican Party has never nominated a woman for major public office. Women first voted in this state in 1920 and it wasn't until 1974 that a female was nominated for a major office—Democrat Helen Bliss of New Ipswich for the Second Congressional District nod. She lost by 30,605 votes to six-term U.S. representative James Cleveland of New London. Since then the Democrats have nominated a woman eleven times for either governor, U.S. senator or for the U.S. House, including three women in 2002.

The closest a woman has come to winning a GOP nomination for any of these offices was Doloris Bridges of Concord, who lost the GOP Senate nod to Second District representative Perkins Bass by just 1,692 votes in an extremely bitter contest in September

1962. This was to fill the remainder of the term of Mrs. Bridges's late husband, Styles, and she enjoyed the vigorous support of William Loeb, just as her husband always had. Bass in turn lost the general election to Democrat Tom McIntyre of Laconia.

The first (and still only) woman to attain a top political office here has been Jeanne Shaheen, who served as state coordinator for Carter's primary effort in 1976 and as campaign director for Colorado senator Gary Hart's winning primary effort in 1984.

Shaheen won the governorship in 1996 by 87,854 votes over Manchester attorney Ovide Lamontagne. That election was one in which one of two barriers had to fall—either the state elected its first woman or the first person of Franco-American descent won a major statewide office. In other words, the barrier for gender or the largest ethnic group had to fall. With Shaheen's victory that means only the barrier to Franco-Americans remains.

The book *In Pursuit of the White House 2000*, edited by William G. Mayer, includes a chapter titled "The Changing Face of the New Hampshire Primary" by Emmett Buell Jr., a professor of political science at Dennison University.

Buell, who has written extensively on the primary, states,

> The media environment in New Hampshire has changed enormously since William Loeb's day. Nackey Loeb took over the paper after William died in 1981 and, with the help of editor Joseph McQuaid, continued her husband's tradition of dyspeptic editorials, shrill headlines, and the full-court press for favored candidates.

I beg to differ. Certainly the paper retains significant clout in shaping the direction of this state, but the claim that it hasn't changed in the past two decades is a subject for debate.

William Loeb was one of a kind, and it is doubtful that American journalism will ever see his likes again—which is something a lot of us will be thankful for. But the type of knife-and-kill journalism that Theodore White laid at the paper's doorstep is very much a thing of the past.

Yet there are times when the paper does show a glimmer of its former self, just as a fading star professional athlete plays a game with the skill he had in years past.

In the year 2002 the paper showed its partisanship (Republican, of course) on behalf of U.S. representative John E. Sununu, who'd represented the First (eastern) District for three terms before defeating two-term U.S. senator Bob Smith in the GOP primary, the first time in the state's history that a senator lost a primary fight.

In the general election the paper turned its attention to Sununu's opponent, three-term Democratic governor Jeanne Shaheen.

While not turning its reporters into gumshoes (a trait all too prevalent in Loeb's heyday), almost every day the paper took out after Shaheen, and Representative Sununu defeated Governor Shaheen by 19,751 votes (4.4%), once again leaving every major seat in the hands of the GOP.

In 2000 Governor Shaheen won a third term by defeating Republican former U.S. senator (1979–1991) Gordon Humphrey by just 4.9%. She managed to win the state's largest county—Hillsborough—which happens to contain the two largest cities (Manchester and Nashua) by 3,455 votes.

Yet after failing to enact a state sales tax in 2001 (which the *Union Leader*, to no one's surprise, strongly opposed), she lost Hillsborough County by 10,966 votes to Sununu. This turned out to be one of the closest Senate races in the nation and the Senate is now in the hands of the GOP by just two seats.

Anyone studying the last two elections can only conclude that the Loeb legacy played a significant role in determining which party controls not just the U.S. Senate, but also the White House.

III

PERSON-TO-PERSON

Polls have almost completely supplanted any substantive dia-
logue between either reporters and the public or the candidate and
voters.

The result is that the media and the two parties now hold
their own elections. If it has anything to do with us, our problems
or the issues we see around us, that isn't clear. The significance
attached to New Hampshire itself vividly illustrates this. Media
folklore portrays the state as the last repository of old-fashioned
individualism, where voters aren't afraid to tell presidents where
to get off. It is, in fact, the very unpredictability that gives the primary so much power and supplies the rationale for so much coverage. It's a brilliant hustle—without it, who would ever pay attention at all?

—Jon Katz, *Rolling Stone*, April 16, 1992

HAVING MOVED TO THE GRANITE STATE in the spring of 1969, after
spending the winter in California I returned the following
spring to settle here permanently.

In early August 1971 I joined the staff of the GOP presidential
campaign of Rep. Pete McCloskey of California, who was chal-
lenging President Richard Nixon. McCloskey reaped just 20%
here; he thus failed to launch a Gene McCarthy–style uprising
against a president and he returned to California, where he won a
fourth term in Congress.

Realizing that the New Hampshire GOP was not very receptive to any sort of progressive agenda, I became a Democrat and by

September 1972 had managed to win election as Merrimack County Democratic chairman at the advanced age of 24.

One of the more interesting national Democratic Party leaders I got to know during my two-year tenure as county chairman was former governor of North Carolina and then president of Duke University Terry Sanford.

In 1973 Sanford was chairman of the Democratic Charter Commission and held a hearing in the senate chambers in the State House in Concord. Later, on a trip to Florida, I stopped in to visit with Sanford at the rather palatial home provided to him as president of Duke University.

In the summer of 1974 Sanford asked me to arrange a series of small kaffeeklatsches and I did this in several communities in the Second Congressional District.

While in Concord Sanford was accompanied by Spencer Oliver, the former chairman of the Young Democrats of America. Just two years earlier Oliver had tumbled inadvertently into the pages of history: While he was executive director of the Association of State Democratic Chairmen his phone was tapped, along with that of Democratic National chairman Larry O'Brien, by the Watergate burglars.

While the three of us drove out to the town of Dunbarton, to the west of the state capital of Concord, I was taken aback when Sanford mentioned to me that if he were a competitor in the 1976 New Hampshire primary he felt he could count on the quiet backing of former Democratic governor John King, who was the first person to serve three straight two-year terms in that office, from 1963 to 1969.

King (who died in August 1996) had been appointed to the New Hampshire Superior Court by his successor, Republican governor Walter Peterson, in 1969 and to the state Supreme Court in 1979 by Governor Hugh Gallen, a Democrat. (Gallen later promoted King to chief justice of the state Supreme Court in 1981; he served in that post until his retirement in 1986.)

I thought it might not be proper for a Superior Court justice to be providing advice to a potential presidential candidate, no matter how good friends the two were, but I'm certain this wasn't the first time such a conversation had been held in this country.

I'm certain I did not bring up any questions or concerns about whether Judge King had violated judicial ethics by having contact with Terry Sanford about a possible bid for the White House. However, I did express to Sanford (who was later elected to a single term in the U.S. Senate in 1986) my opinion about how limited a factor King was in New Hampshire Democratic politics.

Although I had not lived here while King was governor, I was always a bit puzzled as I worked on campaigns, served as county chairman, and occasionally wrote about politics, about how limited a force King was.

Governor King had managed to be a Democrat in name only—he had little interest in building a stronger Democratic Party structure and he had gained the reputation among many party activists of being a loner.

Joni Salvas, who has played an active role in many Democratic campaigns, including that of Rep. Morris Udall of Arizona in the 1976 primary, stated in an interview in March 1979 about King: "He kept it in the self-interest of John King. People weren't allowed to put a bumper sticker for Tom McIntyre on their car. When you have a self-centered, self-interested group it's not a Democratic machine. It was a King machine and there's a difference."

John William King was elected governor in 1962, in perhaps the most tumultuous political year in the history of New Hampshire. The victory by 40,914 votes was the first time in four decades that the Democrats had captured the corner office in Concord. It was a victory aided in no small measure by an endorsement of King by two-term GOP governor Wesley Powell, who failed to win his party's nomination.

(The previous Democratic governor was Fred Brown of

Somersworth, an attorney who was a former major league catcher for the Boston Braves who appeared in just seven games in 1901 and two in 1902. Brown lost his bid for reelection in 1924 by 12,959 votes to John Winant and later won a term in the U.S. Senate in 1932.)

King was born in Manchester, the fourth of seven children of Michael and Ann King, both of whom had emigrated from County Mayo, Ireland. His father was a fireman and an engineer.

Following graduation from St. Joseph's High School in Manchester in 1934, he attended Harvard, where his classmates included writer Theodore White; Arthur Schlesinger Jr., who later was an assistant to President John Kennedy; and Kennedy's older brother, Joseph P. Kennedy Jr. He received his degree in 1938.

The future governor then went on to receive his law degree from Columbia Law School in 1944 and by 1948 he returned to the city of his birth to practice law, served in the state legislature from 1957 to 1963 and became an instructor in business law at Saint Anselm College.

Martin Gross, who served as legal counsel to King's successor, Republican Walter Peterson, from 1970 to 1972 and as a special counsel to Democratic governor Hugh Gallen in 1982, said about King: "I think John King did not forget his roots yet John King did have some very interesting roots. An Irish boy from Manchester who nevertheless was educated at Harvard and Columbia Law School. He had a very, very high class education. He had labor connections, he was an anticorporate populist and yet he had carried a pretty good intellectual cargo."

In his memoir *1968 • McCarthy • New Hampshire*, author David Hoeh, who cochaired the state campaign for Eugene McCarthy in that primary, wrote,

> I knew that Manchester would be exceedingly difficult to organize for Senator McCarthy. I had been involved in several political efforts in Manchester and understood its political

dynamics. I had worked in John King's first campaign for governor in 1962 and had watched King fashion a winning coalition from his friends, relatives, political associates, labor contacts, social and ethnic groups. Manchester is the melting pot that never quite melted and has a club, group, church, or association for each of its many immigrant peoples. Its politics revolve around associations and their leadership.

In the 1962 gubernatorial contest, as Martin Gross recalled,

> In that first campaign he knocked John Pillsbury, who was the Republican candidate, in the head by running I would call a classist campaign, by associating Pillsbury with the power of Public Service Co. of New Hampshire (Pillsbury's employer) appealing to what I call the right-wing populism of New Hampshire. He maintained that individualist premise—kind of a tough-minded independent type of guy for the remainder of his years in government.
>
> He could be a tough guy, attack his opponent, characterize his opponent and define his opponent, which is how he dealt with the bunk of the biennium that Republicans put up against him.

The state of Iowa has 99 counties (which should give you an idea of what it is like to wage a statewide campaign there); the Granite State has only 10. Yet it still took Governor King almost six years to get around to addressing the Sullivan County Democratic Committee on Jan. 30, 1968—not until his final full year in office, about six weeks before the Democratic voters had to choose between President Lyndon Johnson and Sen. Eugene McCarthy.

New Hampshire and Vermont are the only states left with two-year terms for governor. In this state the governor is always a serious contender for the award for the weakest governor in the nation. Once a governor departs from office what influence he had is essentially gone. And if appointed to a judgeship as King was, his power in the political arena is virtually eliminated. So the message was conveyed to Terry Sanford on that ride in 1974 that if he was looking for a power broker to help advance his prospects in the next primary he should look elsewhere.

Asked to provide his view of what kind of governor John King had been, Bill Treat opined,

> He had a lot of support from the Dunfey family; they were both very close and I think that was of great help to him. Like a lot of New Hampshire governors he was passing good. If you had to pick out great New Hampshire governors actually I would go back to Sherman Adams, who I think was a great New Hampshire governor. He was the first full-time governor New Hampshire ever had.

One reason the national media and political elite have some problems with understanding what makes the first primary state tick is the fact that this state is, by design as much as by accident, a power vacuum.

Once a presidential contender (especially a Democratic one) begins to comprehend this fact of life, it usually requires those politicians more comfortable with megastate politics in places like California, Texas and New York to do some reprogramming. This is never an easy chore, particularly for leaders who have already reached a high level of prominence and certainly wonder why the blueprint used in the past isn't applicable in such a small state as New Hampshire.

With the governor having to face the electorate every other year the chief executive is in a constant state of campaign preparation or actually campaigning and simply doesn't have enough time to develop policies and programs.

The state also maintains a remnant from colonial times, a five-person Governor's Council, a body that approves state contracts over $2,500, judicial appointments and top state department appointments; thus it's a check on gubernatorial excess if there ever was one.

Yet the governor of this state is provided the opportunity just about every quadrennium to step onto the national stage, and two men have been able to use their position in the corner office to win a promotion to just a few steps from the Oval Office. Sherman Adams left after the end of his second term to become the assistant to the president, Dwight Eisenhower. He was called that because Eisenhower was quoted as saying, "I think of Adams as my chief of staff, but I don't call him that because the politicians think it sounds too military." And John H. Sununu served as President George H. W. Bush's chief of staff from January 1989 until December 1991.

An ongoing study by Dr. Thad Beyle of the University of North Carolina at Chapel Hill ranks the power of each governor. This power rating examines six areas including appointment, budget, veto power, party control, tenure and the number of other statewide elected officials. As more evidence of the embrace of minimalist governance that this state holds so dear, New Hampshire ranks 44th in the nation in the power rating for the year 2001.

In the 13 primaries that have been conducted here since 1952, nine of the Democrats who have emerged victorious have been from the Sunbelt and only four have resided in the Frostbelt.

There is no better evidence to indicate how willing and able the Democratic voters of this state have been to roll out the welcome mat to candidates from other regions of the nation, particularly the South. This is another indication that it is not just the Republicans here who are receptive to aspirants with a more minimalist approach toward government—often at odds with the rest of the Northeast, with its high state and local tax burdens and therefore more extensive and expensive government programs.

Various political analysts and scientists can trot out any number of theories as to why Americans vote the way they do in presidential elections; this observer winnows the process down to essentially a single theory. Once the two major parties have determined their nominee, the single strongest determinant of who'll be president is the candidate's distance from Washington, D.C.

You have to track back as far as 1964 when the ultimate Washington insider and power broker, President Lyndon Johnson, defeated Sen. Barry Goldwater of Arizona in a landslide; Goldwater, as you may recall, had mused about the merits of sawing off the eastern seaboard from the rest of the country. That was the last time a Washington insider trumped the outsider. (Senator Goldwater was quoted on Sept. 30, 1961, telling the *Chicago Tribune*, "Sometimes I think this country would be better off if we could just saw off the Eastern Seaboard and let it float out to sea.")

Since then in election after election in contrasting brief profiles of the two major candidates—present position (being a governor is a major plus), length of time in public service (the shorter the better), and his party's attitude toward the role of government (the less the better), the candidate more closely identified with Washington, D.C., is less likely to win the presidency.

Compare Vice President Al Gore's four terms in the U.S. House, his six years in the Senate and two terms as vice president with Gov. George Bush's six years of elective office. This theory holds up even if the eventual winner of the presidency receives fewer popular votes.

In an interview for the documentary program "Sherman Adams: Yankee Governor," the former attorney general of the United States in the Eisenhower administration, Herbert Brownell, commented on one reason Adams was selected to serve in the role of top assistant:

Eisenhower had great respect for governors. Whenever you mentioned governor so-and-so he would always prick up his ears [as] though that was a most important fellow. So I think it would have been easy to sell Eisenhower on the fact that if he had a governor on his train or as his assistant he had the right man.

It's a curious thing but it was important in understanding how he dealt in the early days of his presidency with political leaders. . . . [asked whether Eisenhower's respect for Adams would have been the same if he had been Sen. Sherman Adams]: It would not have been as important in Eisenhower's view.

As an example of the clout a governor has, since the names of the presidential candidates have been on the ballot commencing in 1952, only two governors have failed to bring home a winner with their endorsement. The first was Republican Meldrim Thomson in 1976, whose candidate, former California governor Ronald Reagan, lost to President Gerald Ford by just 1,587 votes. Another Republican governor, Steve Merrill, saw his choice, Sen. Bob Dole of Kansas, lose by 2,136 votes to commentator Pat Buchanan in 1996.

(Former Democratic governor Jeanne Shaheen was narrowly able to avoid being included in this group; the candidate she backed in the 2000 primary, Vice President Al Gore, defeated former New Jersey senator Bill Bradley by 6,395 votes, a margin of just 4.1%.)

Much of the media fixation in 1991 was on New York Democratic governor Mario Cuomo, mostly speculation about whether he would finally make up his mind and attempt to move from the banks of the Hudson River to those of the Potomac.

Every once in a while an article would pop up as an early warning signal that all was not well in Albany, where Cuomo was ensconced in his third and what would turn out to be his final term as governor of the Empire State. (In November 1990 Cuomo had won with 54% of the vote, at first glance not a landslide until one realizes that the second-place finisher was a Republican who received just 21% and that the candidate of the Conservative Party tallied 20%.)

Sometimes reading the tea leaves does help one determine not only whether someone will announce for the presidency, but what type of candidate he'll probably be if he does run.

There were clues that Governor Cuomo would not be a candidate for president in 1992 despite mountains of press speculation that he would be.

Clearly having some tolerance for life on the road is one requirement for someone seeking the Oval Office. But writing in the *New York Times* on Sept. 22, 1991, reporter Kevin Sack noted some of the activities of the Empire State governor, images that helped to shape the political folklore that surrounds him:

> But few of those images can compete with Mr. Cuomo's obsession with sleeping in his own bed. Of the 3,187 days that Mr. Cuomo has been Governor, he has, by his staff's count, spent only 36 nights away from the Executive Mansion.
>
> As the emerging field of Democratic candidates gathered at the national party's fall meeting in Los Angeles this weekend, those closest to Mr. Cuomo cited his reluctance to travel as one of the reasons he has shied away from a race for the White House. His absence from the meeting and his stay-at-home record may be the most convincing evidence that he is not planning a Presidential campaign, they said.

While all presidents and many governors require a travel office to make arrangements for leaders who seem to be in constant motion, this was not necessary for New York's leader, according to Sack: "As in most years, the Governor's one-week vacation was spent in the Executive Mansion last month, where he could read and work the phones without wearing a suit or making appearances."

The article added, "Andrew Cuomo, the Governor's oldest son and closest adviser, said the infrequency of his father's travels this year—only seven out-of-state trips and one overnighter—demonstrates that he means what he says about not running for President."

By the end of the week the story was published that Cuomo would depart for a week-long trade mission to Japan. Sack: "It will be only the second overseas trip of his three terms as Governor. The first was to the Soviet Union in 1987."

In writing about this lack of wanderlust, columnist David Broder wrote in the *Concord Monitor* on Oct. 22, 1991, "Even when he travels, it is questionable how much he learns, because his habit is to fly back to Albany, even if it takes half the night, as soon as the applause dies."

A review of campaign travel schedules starting with Tennessee senator Estes Kefauver in 1952 through the 2000 primary would no doubt find that virtually all presidential contenders spent at least 36 evenings away from home in just two or three months' time, never mind nine years.

Every once in a while an article or news account appears that goes deeper than the standard coverage of straw and straw-free polls, money raised and spent, endorsements, gaffes and verbal miscues and the like. Sometimes you actually learn some useful information about a would-be president. One such article, titled "Mario's Calling," was written by Jacob Weisberg in the Dec. 2, 1991, issue of *The New Republic*.

Weisberg wrote in part, "National reporters less familiar with Cuomo, however, may be in for a shock if he decides to run. What they will discover is that along with his famed thoughtfulness goes a hypersensitivity to criticism that makes covering him one of the most difficult jobs in journalism."

Weisberg tracked down some of the reporters who had been in turn tracked down by the governor while dining out, while visiting with relatives, or at their own apartments in Albany and even "in the wee hours of the morning."

The bureau chief for the *New York Times* in the mid-'80s was quoted as saying, "He sounded like a man not in control of his temper, paranoid, beside himself." The article also noted that "Cuomo enjoys hectoring journalists and still cannot always resist the urge to do so."

Another reporter was quoted as saying, "There are times when it will start pleasant. There will be a pretense of something else. But there will be something irking him. And he will start to scream."

If Governor Cuomo had run in 1992 he would not have had to deal with William Loeb. But there would have been row after row of journalists not just from the *Union Leader* and other news services in the Granite State, but also the Boston media, which rarely pays attention to its neighboring state to the north until the presidential primary rolls around and the opportunity to use it as a platform for greater regional and national notoriety arrives.

Thus the pressure cooker analogy would have been applicable and given Cuomo's inexperience as a national candidate his first attempt at being one had enormous potential to fall far short of the expectations his candidacy would have received from so many in the Democratic Party across the nation.

One trademark of every primary is the onslaught of polls unleashed on the public by a variety of media outlets—with television stations often in the lead.

According to an Associated Press account published in the *Concord Monitor* on Nov. 13, 1991, in a survey of 469 registered Democrats and Independents, New York governor Mario Cuomo had 30% of definite or probable voters for the Feb. 18 Democratic primary. In second place was former Bay State senator Paul Tsongas with 10%. In sixth place, with just 4%, was the eventual nominee, Arkansas governor Bill Clinton, who trailed even former California governor Jerry Brown by a point.

It would be nice if in divulging this information media operations and polling firms provided the public with some context for their latest polling production. If these polls have such merit, why not remind the public of any similar poll conducted a quadrennium before, and the accuracy of its measurement of the public's pulse. Of course, if this was actually done the grain of salt such surveys are taken with would grow to the size of the massive salt piles located at Portsmouth Harbor to help clear the roads in a northern New England winter.

These surveys almost without exception measure the recognition level of the possible and actual contenders and quadrennium in and quadrennium out have little relevance to the final outcome.

However, they do have an impact on fundraising, recruitment of support, endorsements, media attention and sometimes who finally decides to become a candidate. But perhaps if the public had a broader understanding of what these surveys mean now and what they've meant in the past, the quality of the candidate and his ideas, abilities and experiences would count for more than they do now.

Say what you will about the numerous flaws and drawbacks of our nomination system, it still does have its value. One important one is that it forces the candidates out of the comfortable confines of their offices largely on Capitol Hill and into the hinterlands.

When campaigning in locations such as Iowa and New Hampshire, both at some but not a great distance from the nation's capital, the hopefuls interact with the public more than they otherwise would.

Governors already do this interacting to a much greater extent than members of the U.S. Senate or House, and that helps explain why six out of the last seven presidential contests have been won by governors or former governors. (Only Warren Harding of Ohio in 1920 and John Kennedy of Massachusetts in 1960 have ever gone directly from the Senate to the presidency. And only James Garfield, who served in the U.S. House from 1863 to 1880, moved directly from that body to the presidency; he had been appointed to the Senate in 1880 but did not serve there before ascending to the presidency.)

Many years ago David Powers, who was with John Kennedy in 1946 during his first race for public office (the Democratic nomination to the 11th congressional district in and around Boston) and later became the curator for the Kennedy Library, was reminiscing about the 1960 primary in West Virginia.

This state proved to be the gateway to the nomination; Kennedy, a Catholic, managed to defeat Minnesota senator Hubert Humphrey by 84,300 votes in a heavily Protestant state.

Powers talked about what it was like to campaign in a place that had so much poverty and where its major industry, coal mining, was such a difficult and dangerous way to make a living.

His comment, that Kennedy was a different individual after he emerged from the coal mines he had ventured into, spoke volumes about the value of men who are so often beneficiaries of privilege having to seek out support from those living and working in conditions that would never be described as privileged.

Any system of presidential nomination that reinforces the need for candidates to take the time and effort to actually see with their own eyes how Americans get through their day deserves preservation.

It is not a myth that the populace of the Granite State manages to get close and personal in interacting with the presidential wannabes. Yet not everyone takes advantage of every opportunity presented to meet possibly the next president of the United States.

For example, during the winter of 1970 and 1971, I was living at the Nashua residence of architect Bliss Woodruff and his wife, Marian, who was the director of education for the Currier Gallery in Manchester.

On the evening of Feb. 25, 1971, the Woodruffs asked me whether I'd be attending the reception they would be hosting the following morning for Sen. George McGovern. I told them that since I'd already heard McGovern speak to a group of students at Nathaniel Hawthorne College in Antrim earlier that day I would rather sleep in than attend the reception downstairs.

McGovern had announced his candidacy in Washington, D.C., on Jan. 18 and this would be his initial visit to the first primary state as an official candidate.

It is understood that with the advent of television regional accents are gradually disappearing. For those who appreciate the diversity of speech of a nation as complex as this, the loss of such diversity is mourned. But there are times when someone's sound is, to put it kindly, grating.

As McGovern began to speak to this group of about 100 college students I was taken aback by how pronounced his Midwestern nasal twang was. Indeed, it was so pronounced that my reaction was a rather strong sinking feeling in my stomach—not to mention the disappointment that someone seeking the highest office in the land had such an obvious ability to grate on one's nerves.

During the speech I was standing next to Charles Officer of Hanover, the Democratic nominee in the Second Congressional District in 1964 (and again in 1974, both times losing to Republican Jim Cleveland), to see whether he was having the same adverse reaction I was. Nope. Officer went on to serve as McGovern's state chairman.

So the event starting at 8:00 A.M. listed on McGovern's sched-

ule as a "Breakfast with Nashua Democratic leaders" at the impos-
ing 10,000-square-foot Woodruff residence with 10 bedrooms and
7 baths constructed in 1901 in the exclusive North End section of
Nashua went on while this observer slept upstairs.

In November 1972 the Democratic presidential nominee, Sen.
George McGovern of South Dakota, won only two of the thirteen
cities in New Hampshire. (President Nixon won the state with
64.1% of the vote.) McGovern narrowly won the city of
Somersworth near the border with Maine, and the North Country
city of Berlin. He lost the Upper Valley community of Claremont
by just 35 votes; however, he was slammed in Manchester with just
31.6% (his worst showing in a city) and in the capital of Concord
his 36% was his second worst city performance in the state.

In the last century the Democratic nominee for president carried the state only eight times: 1912 (by 1,797 votes), 1916 (by 56
votes), 1936, 1940, 1944, 1964, 1992 and 1996.

In November 1991 Arkansas governor Bill Clinton toured the
city of Claremont with state representative Peter Burling of
Cornish, who then represented a district of four towns to the north
of Claremont. (At the time he was also Sullivan County
Democratic chairman and he has served as the House minority
leader since late 1996.)

In the biography of John McLane Clark's all-too-brief life,
author David Bradley in *Journey of a Johnny-Come-Lately* (published
by Dartmouth Publications in 1957) describes the city of Claremont,
where Clark owned and operated the *Claremont Daily Eagle*:

> Claremont, New Hampshire, is nothing if it is not a typi-
> cal northern New England mill town—in New England, typi-
> cal is nothing if it is not individual. Old, isolated, durable,
> slow, reasonably content, Claremont lies in a pocket of hills
> above the Connecticut River. Built on this upland bench for the
> water power provided by the modest Sugar River, Claremont

began its industrial history in textiles and shoes more than a hundred years ago. The town has been remodeled economically many times yet it looks today very much the same as it did just after the Civil War. Its public buildings, hotels, and shops cluster around the central square—dark red brick in the extreme Manchester-Pawtucket style. Its ancient factories wind down along the banks of the Sugar River, although no one would think of using water power any more.

While being driven to Claremont by Burling, the future president was briefed about the local economy, which was in decline with the loss of manufacturing jobs. One company holding on was the American Brush Company, which produced paintbrushes and rollers. Clinton told Burling the company should contact Wal-Mart, a company of which his wife, Hillary, was on the board of directors, and attempt to tap into their Buy American campaign and see whether it would be possible to generate more orders and therefore more employment in Claremont.

On Jan. 31, 1992, the *Boston Globe* ran an article by Michael Frisby that noted that Clinton's efforts on behalf of this company had critics charging that it "amounts to the candidate swapping jobs for support from local officials and voters."

It seems that the mayor at the time, Raymond Gagnon, had been leaning toward supporting Iowa senator Tom Harkin. However, when the president of the company followed Clinton's suggestion for the company to contact "my guys," this time Wal-Mart's response was more receptive.

The article included an observation from one former Sullivan County Democratic chair, saying, "she does not blame Claremont officials, but that she thinks it was 'disreputable' of Clinton to use such tactics in what she said was a bid to get votes" and added " 'Claremont is a beggar town. If someone is going to hand you a few bucks, are you going to say no?' "

One could ask why it was necessary for the governor of Arkansas to try to be the catalyst in bringing more jobs to the New Hampshire city of Claremont. The problem of loss of mill jobs has plagued other communities—especially others without easy access to the interstate highway system, in particular those in the North Country.

It is another matter altogether in the four southern and eastern counties—Strafford, Rockingham, Merrimack and Hillsborough counties; in the past half-century this region has been one of the fastest growing areas in the Northeast.

Yet once in a while someone from the remote North Country is elected governor, as Democrat Hugh Gallen was in 1978 and then again two years later. Gallen, from the town of Littleton, just to the north of Franconia Notch in the White Mountains, used his position to try to lure as many companies northward as he could.

After Gallen was defeated by Sununu (Gallen died on Dec. 29, 1982, in a Boston hospital shortly before he was to leave office), during Sununu's tenure I was visiting with the publisher of the local weekly in Littleton and asked him if the new governor was doing as much for the local economy as the late governor had done.

The publisher responded by mentioning that Sununu had given a speech not long before to a local group and he was asked what ideas he had for adding more jobs to the local economy.

Sununu's response was to inform the group that they should send someone down to the World Trade Center and start knocking on doors in order to drum up new businesses.

The newspaper publisher conveyed the message that his reaction was shared by others in attendance—that such an effort would not prove to be the salvation for the economic vitality of the distant town of Littleton.

It was unusual for a Democrat to carry the state not just once but twice, as Clinton did in 1992 and 1996. The severe economic downturn in the late '80s and early '90s was so deep it could be referred to as the Great Recession and was a major reason Clinton was able to carry the state twice.

The political leader who was the state's chief executive during this downturn was Judd Gregg, now the state's senior senator. He told John Gfroerer in the documentary on the New Hampshire primary, "The Premier Primary,"

> We were in the worst downturn since arguably the depression and possibly even competitive with the depression in New Hampshire.
>
> Five of our seven largest banks had closed, our two major public utilities had gone bankrupt, housing prices had dropped thirty to sixty percent, state revenues had dropped for thirty-six straight months from month to month—we were in a devastated state and he [Bush] was president.

Also, Clinton's indefatigable campaigning paid off in such a small state where the grip-and-grin approach can make a difference if enough time and energy are expended (something that can't be replicated in a megastate). And unlike President Jimmy Carter (another master of the grip-and-grin school), who did not play close attention to the Democratic Party and matters of patronage appointments, Clinton was far superior at attending to such matters.

Sometimes candidates and how they campaign seem interchangeable and sometimes they do not. The following written about Gov. George Bush by Jill Zuckman in the Nov. 5, 1999 issue of the *Boston Globe* would never have one confusing George W. Bush for Bill Clinton: "And while McCain has concentrated his efforts on answering voters' questions at town-hall style forums, Bush has limited his question-and-answer sessions. In Littleton, Tuesday night at the Elks Lodge, the governor took six questions before deciding it was time to quit.

" 'Two more questions, then I got to go to bed,' Bush said. It was 7:40 P.M."

Does the voters' clearly established interest in the presidential candidate with the greatest distance from Washington sometimes mean that they want someone with no political experience?

Since Gen. Dwight Eisenhower was sworn in as president on Jan. 20, 1953, no one without some degree of elective experience has managed to gain the presidency.

Since then the individual who has come closest to winning the White House without any record of public office was Texas businessman H. Ross Perot. He tallied 19% of the vote in 1992 and 8% in 1996.

Because Perot never held an elective position, the news media would have had to devote some attention to his business record to provide their readers and viewers a sense of what type of president Perot might be. It was up to the press to find out what his abilities and limitations were. However, like so much else with the major media and the reduced attention and resources devoted to politics and public policy in this nation, the coverage of Perot left something to be desired.

The June 1992 issue of *Texas Monthly* magazine published an article with the title "Ross and Me: It is good to have Ross Perot as my business partner—most days." The lead-in to the article was:

What is it like to do a deal with H. Ross Perot? In early 1988 a 29-year-old inventor from Austin named Steve McElroy had a patent pending on a one-size-fits-all lid for cups, cans, and other food containers. But to get his invention to market, he needed a savvy partner. He decided that he wanted Perot. Three days after McElroy mailed a letter to Perot he received a call from Perot himself. For the next three and a half years McElroy kept letters and notes of his dealings with Perot, as their partnership flourished and floundered and Perot put McElroy to test after test.

A great deal of what one reads in various magazines is quickly forgotten. This first-person account did not fall into that category. The theme of the article was (without using those words) that Ross Perot was a control freak. And the conclusion that one could readily reach (and that the author with his need to retain Perot as his partner did not go near) was that someone so ready to give McElroy so many different tests (or torture or torment if the truth be told) would never manage to operate the Oval Office.

Prior to McElroy's initial meeting on March 1, 1988, to discuss with Perot his invention called the Total Top, a stretchable lid to fit over containers of all shapes and sizes, over the phone Perot proclaimed it to be "a world-class idea."

Their first conclave was a bit rocky; after just five minutes of discussion Perot proclaimed the meeting over and tossed the young inventor out of his Dallas office. But he really hadn't done that, for it was merely a test that McElroy managed to pass. Yet the inventor was discovering that "there would always be a fine line between pleasing and displeasing Perot."

Later McElroy became alarmed at his wealthy partner's "intransigent position" opposing trying to become partners with one of the largest paper cup companies in the world. When that met a dead-end Perot made an effort to buy his partner out. That was just as difficult as anything else for when a disclosure of who the company was attempting to buy out Perot would not be revealed to him he proclaimed, "Well, we don't have any more to discuss then. This deal is dead. Thank you."

The nomination process is the sole device the nation has to learn more about the eventual nominees of the two major parties. Since we don't have a parliamentary system that utilizes peer review to elevate leaders to its upper ranks and then finally to the position of prime minister for the party that achieves a plurality, we are left with a much different way to find our top national leader. We certainly don't have an institution of higher learning to train our presidents and surely there are few in the nation who would contend that four years in the vice presidency would have been ample time for Dan Quayle to prepare to become the president of the United States.

The American focus on someone like Perot is not the first time recently that there has been an electoral fascination for a prominent and wealthy entrepreneur: Remember the buildup for Donald Trump in 1988 and Lee Iacocca in 1984?

In the end our presidential elections are like so much else in life—a compromise. We won't entrust the White House to a powerful business leader. In my interview published in the *New Hampshire Times* on Jan. 28, 1976, Arizona congressman Morris Udall stated,

> There's no real preparation, there's no place you can go to get a certificate that you're qualified to administer the federal government. I guess Nelson Rockefeller, Ronald Reagan and the president of General Motors have the biggest administrative ability of anybody in the country and I wouldn't want any one of them within five miles of residence in the White House.

Another troubling aspect of media coverage of the Perot phenomenon was how scant the reporting and analysis was of how he would manage his administration's relations with Congress. Perot's strong-willed, driven and stubborn qualities—all necessary to building a successful business—would no doubt have been of little value to this political novice in trying to deal with the grand panjandrums on Capitol Hill.

After reading the *Texas Monthly* account I began to keep an eye out for when it would become part of the mix of media reports about the Perot candidacy for president.

Since Perot had brought his very own political party into the race there wasn't any connection between this Texas billionaire and the 1992 or 1996 New Hampshire primaries. But he was surely a factor in the general election as he entered, withdrew from and then reentered the race. He received in 1992 the strongest showing for a third-party candidate since former president Theodore Roosevelt's Progressive Party bid in 1912, which garnered 27%.

However, as the campaign progressed I could find nothing on this business partnership. Since Perot had never held, or even run for, political office, I was certain some reporters who read *Texas Monthly* (which currently has a circulation of 300,000), would read the article and use it as a way to analyze whether Perot had what it takes to handle our top national office.

Yet no matter how many articles were written about him or how many times Perot showed up on TV to display his charts and to become a seemingly constant guest on one particular TV talk show, I never came across anything on what it was like to be a partner of his and to try to develop the product called the Total Top.

Although it is a small item and there is surely more to judge Perot on than this one business partnership, it says something about the breadth and depth of the coverage of his candidacy that this eight-page article never again came to my notice.

(In an attempt to see whether something was missed, I made a visit to the New Hampshire State Library to check the index of the *New York Times* to see whether in 1992 there was any mention of Perot's partner. Not a one.)

Near the end of his account Steve McElroy wrote,

> I wanted to stay in business with Perot. He had put me through a lot, made me jump through a lot of hoops to stay where I had wanted to be, but somehow I didn't take any of it personally. Perot, I now understood, made decisions based solely on his business judgment. He expected no less from those with whom he dealt. Working with Perot was the ultimate challenge and exhilaration. I wanted to learn more.

McGovern's national campaign manager in 1972 was Gary Hart, who would win a Senate seat from Colorado in 1974, narrowly win reelection in 1980 and mount his own bid for the 1984 Democratic presidential nomination, only to lose a close fight to Walter Mondale.

Several weeks before the Feb. 28, 1984 vote in the first primary Senator Hart conducted a press conference in his state headquarters in Bicentennial Square in downtown Concord. About 10 reporters were in attendance and during the session a columnist for *New Hampshire Profiles* asked the senator to reflect on what it was like to be raised on the plains of Kansas. It was obvious from the expression of disdain on Hart's face and his rather curt answer that he did not want to respond to that question, so the press conference quickly returned to a Q-and-A revolving around the issues with nil about his upbringing.

Hart's background probably falls somewhere between the idyllic upbringing that scions from wealthy families such as Franklin Roosevelt, John Kennedy and both the presidential Bushes enjoyed, and the dysfunctional upbringing in the family-from-hell that Bill Clinton had to endure. But for Hart to blow the question off with such coldness and abruptness did leave one wondering not whether Hart had something to hide but whether he simply felt he had better ways to use his time than to dwell on his own past.

With the media's emphasis on celebrity, it is obvious that candidates do have to reveal more than their position papers. Talking to some degree about one's upbringing and life does provide some clues about the character and personality that emerge first to the reporters covering the candidate and then to the voters who determine his or her fate.

In a state in northern New England weather can have an impact on the outcome, particularly if it snows on election day and depresses the turnout, thus affecting the results.

In her book Sue Casey wrote,

> Despite the doom and gloom that seemed to pervade so much of the campaign, the sun always shone when Hart was campaigning in New Hampshire. Literally. Hart had been traveling to New Hampshire for an entire year, had been in the state on more than fifty days, and it had never snowed or stormed during his visits. Planes had never been grounded, events had never been canceled because of bad weather, roads had never been too slippery. Hart had never had to campaign during winter blizzards or spring downpours—not on his first trip in December of 1982 nor on his announcement day in February of 1983, not in the early spring when he hiked on the top of Mt. Washington. On those days skies were blue, the sun bright, the air unusually warm. I called them Hart days.

What an omen all that sunny weather turned out to be—the vote in 1984 became yet another stunning upset in a place that has seen more than its share of such outcomes. Omens were in abundance during that same primary in 1984, for it seemed that whenever former Florida governor Reubin Askew campaigned in the winter a snowstorm accompanied him; he finished in ninth place with just 1,025 votes, trailing even the write-in for President Reagan by 4,033 votes.

(It should be noted that at a July 1983 Manchester City Democratic Committee picnic Askew managed to draw 1,066 votes in a straw vote—41 more than he tallied on Feb. 28. That strong showing in Manchester was largely attributed to the presence of many Amway distributors supporting the former Florida governor who were in the area for a convention.)

(That result should have been sufficient to end once and for all this nation's political system of any and all straw votes, but, alas, although such silly exercises are in decline, they still persist, particularly in the Hawkeye State.)

As the candidates were laying the groundwork for their bids in 1988 several announced in early 1987. One was Hart, who threw his hat into the ring in Colorado on April 14. In late January he had been in Concord, speaking to a group at the Legislative Office Building (LOB).

A few months before, I had read Casey's book and since this was the first time I'd seen her since doing so I complimented her on what she had published. While standing outside the LOB room where Hart was to speak, I quipped to her that I hoped the weather that day was not an omen of things to come. It happened to be one of those days that so many people in this region dread—there was more ice than snow or rain in the atmosphere and it could only be considered one type of weather—Askew weather.

Casey, perhaps aware of all that was to follow with Hart's second bid soon thereafter, did not even look at me when I commented that I hoped the dreadful weather was not a sign of trouble down the road.

Yet sure enough, on May 4 the *Miami Herald* disclosed that Hart had been spending time with model Donna Rice and five days later, after failing to stanch the flow of controversy over allegations of womanizing, Hart was out of the race.

The Colorado senator dropped back into the race in mid-December, stating that it was a matter to "let the people decide," yet this time around in 1988 he was in Askew country as far as his vote was concerned, finishing seventh with just 4% of the vote.

An article I wrote, published in the *Concord Monitor* on March 15, 1984, follows:

"Not an accurate portrayal of our primary's history"

The day after the [1984] New Hampshire primary two reporters for the *Boston Globe* proclaimed [that] the best election night coverage was provided by WCBV-TV, Channel 5 in Boston. According to Jack Thomas and Ed Siegel of the *Globe*, the station "covered every candidate, provided the most thorough reporting and presented the most cogent analysis."

Channel 5 may in fact deserve such a bouquet. Yet one of its earlier primary programs, a half-hour special titled "The First Step," aired Feb. 12, set a new standard for inaccurate reporting on the presidential primary.

The first part of the program was devoted to brief segments covering four sections of the state: The Monadnock region, the North Country, Manchester and the Seacoast.

This observer had already seen longer versions of the Monadnock and Manchester reports on Channel 5 evening broadcasts. Compared to other out-of-state attempts to cover this primary they contained a minimum of mistakes.

There is, however, an uncontrollable desire to portray this state as the Mississippi of the North. This penchant seems to begin with a certain daily newspaper in Boston, and is then picked up by the Boston television stations and thereafter other metropolitan and national news media outlets. Therefore the Granite State is saddled with a label it does not always deserve.

This desire to pin the state into a corner populated only by a Far Right fringe necessitates fabricating the news, as reporter Clark Booth did on "The First Step," rather than reporting it.

Booth went out on a search-and-destroy mission, commencing with the slogan on New Hampshire's license plates. He stated, "Most states have a slogan, usually something cheerful to stoke tourism. New Hampshire has a warning, framed almost like an epithet, 'Live Free or Die.' That is the motto."

A discourse on the stridently nationalistic tone of the slogan followed and Booth said, "It speaks to a theme that New Hampshire has long espoused since long, long before she took to wearing her nationalism on her number plates." There is, said Booth, "something in the chill here," something that "expresses that shrill echo New Hampshire gives to the provocative term—patriotism—it has always been so."

In examining the roots of rampant nationalism Booth took a look at the era of Sen. Joseph McCarthy of Wisconsin, who rose to national fame in the late '40s as a zealous combatant of what he perceived to be the communist menace in America.

Of the first New Hampshire primary that provided for a vote on the presidential candidates in 1952, Booth said of the GOP contest between Gen. Dwight Eisenhower and Ohio senator Robert Taft, "In the crucial New Hampshire contest Eisenhower was able to depict himself as more ardently anticommunist than the more conservative Taft. It was a decisive factor." Booth trotted out Roy Cohn, a prominent attorney in New York City and one-time associate of McCarthy, as of all things an authority on the election in 1952. Cohn said, "Eisenhower did pitch his start on certain areas of the country, that of the McCarthy strongly anticommunist position, which was extremely strong in places like New England and a number of other areas in the country."

In fact the matter of McCarthyism was no factor at all in the outcome of the Eisenhower–Taft contest here in 1952. Eisenhower never made one political statement during that primary. He was serving in a military position in France, commanding the organizing of the armed forces of NATO. He was prohibited by Army regulations from making any political statements or engaging in any political activity. Eisenhower did not return from France until early June, just as the primary campaign was concluding.

Still Booth continued with his fabrication, "New Hampshire rose to McCarthy's bait 32 years ago, allowing him to profoundly influence that first primary. But they were not alone for it was happening everywhere else in the country, too.

"Still, it's also a fact that nagging reserves of McCarthyism prevail here today in more virile deposits than you'll find elsewhere. It's the appeal of simple solutions that tends to flourish where there is greater calm and detachment."

About the only accurate comment Booth managed to make during this report was "New Hampshire is never predictable," something confirmed Feb. 28.

While Channel 5's own promotions bill it as the station that provided "the most comprehensive coverage in the New Hampshire primary," the fact is that on "The First Step" the station managed to embarrass itself attempting to cover part of the history of the nation's first primary. [end of article]

On Nov. 20, 1981, Ohio senator John Glenn received a warm reception from 600 New Hampshire Democrats gathered at a fundraiser for second-term Democratic governor Hugh Gallen. Since Glenn had so obviously bombed as the keynote speaker at the 1976 Democratic National Convention, he managed to exceed the low expectation level he had to hurdle.

However, one speech does not make a primary campaign and Glenn gave a clear indication of how loose his grasp of national politics was in pulling together a presidential campaign as he allowed a total of 10 months to elapse before he showed up in the Granite State again. Such indifference allowed the other Democratic contenders to sweep through the state pulling into their bids the few hundred Democratic activists available. Therefore, by the time Glenn started to organize it proved to be too late to see whether any sort of lift-off could transpire.

As one author of a book on the primary has written, "But in New Hampshire, day after day, month after month, the candidates cannot hide who they are."

So once Glenn did start to campaign his true self emerged—and it was not a very vivid personality that came on stage.

There are some—Bill Clinton is one—who are naturals at the political arts. He's had a lifetime of campaigning to refine his gifts. John Glenn served in the U.S. Marine Corps from 1942 to 1965, including service in Korea as a fighter pilot. He was an astronaut from 1959 to 1965, on Feb. 20, 1962 becoming the first American to orbit the earth. Therefore, he had a different lifetime of experience from Clinton's before he won a seat in the U.S. Senate in 1974, following two unsuccessful attempts in his native Ohio.

New Hampshire may be a long way from a place like Arkansas, but it seems to have a stronger pull toward Southern politicians—Kefauver, Carter and Clinton—than it does toward Midwesterners.

Asked why John Glenn never achieved lift-off in his presidential effort, Michael Birkner stated: "He had nothing to say . . . on paper he was the strongest Democrat to run against Reagan in 1984. He was a hero, he had a good record in the Senate, he was from an important state, he was a moderate who could presumably hold the party together, but he had nothing to say and he didn't know how to say it."

"I do know that when I met him I thought he [Glenn] was a decent man, I thought he was a nice guy, an intelligent fellow, but I came away from that conversation to this day I still don't know why he wanted to be president of the United States," stated Martin Gross about his one-on-one séance with then-senator Glenn in his law office that overlooks the State House plaza in Concord.

In the interview conducted on Sept. 10, 2002, Gross remembered,

John Glenn came to New Hampshire and for some reason wanted to speak with me. He sat in the seat right there and I sat in the seat you're sitting in. And I said, "Senator, why do you want to be president?" It's the usual softball I lob and I just listen. And the answer I got was not memorable at the time or now.

It did not say to me that he had a clear moral compass that would guide him in the directions that he would go as a person who was in control of my life. And I think that that was why he turned out to be a weak candidate. In the final analysis the successful candidate has to be able to communicate with voters in that way.

It can sometimes come as a surprise that even U.S. senators running for this nation's highest office don't come to the race ready to run.

For example, I attempted to hold a conversation with Delaware senator Joseph Biden in early July 1987, a few months before he dropped out on Sept. 23.

Biden was the guest of a kaffeeklatsch at a private home in the Heights section of Concord. He was meeting and greeting individuals outside a middle-class home when he came up and introduced himself.

We were standing at the end of a short driveway, next to the house. Somewhere the senator had learned that it would help him make an impression on voters if he really took charge of the conversation (probably from a consultant; his candidacy that year surely did not lack them).

The more he talked the more he managed to be in my face, so much so that I was soon backed to the edge of the driveway and if not for a U-turn would have been standing out in the middle of the road. Fortunately the senator was soon summoned into the house to deliver his campaign pitch, which recounted in the great detail only the loquacious Biden can muster concerning the confirmation fight against the nomination of Robert Bork to the Supreme Court of the United States.

On June 26 that year Justice Lewis Powell had announced his retirement from the U.S. Supreme Court, and President Reagan had decided that Robert Bork would be a suitable replacement. The U.S. Senate did not agree and on Oct. 23 by a vote of 58 to 42 told the president to find another nominee.

In an event recorded by C-Span at a home in the town of Unity, in the western part of the state, Biden boasted in response to a question by Frank Fahey, a teacher, about his academic accomplishments, "I think I probably have a much higher I.Q. than you do, I suspect. I went to law school on a full academic scholarship . . ." That kaffeeklatsch occurred on April 7. By August 7 Biden was at it again, this time at the Franklin Pierce Law Center in Concord, yet again with an inaccurate recounting of his law school record.

No one would ever confuse Biden's liberal voting record with that of the late Sen. Barry Goldwater, the GOP nominee in 1964 against President Lyndon Johnson. Yet they do share something in common, for what Theodore White wrote about Goldwater has equal application to the senior senator from Delaware (who was first elected in 1972 at the age of 29): "His candor is the completely unrestrained candor of old men and little children."

Finally, on Sept. 23, 1987, Biden announced his decision to depart the race for the presidency after allegations of plagiarism in his speeches (from a British political leader and from Robert Kennedy) along with the inaccuracies about his achievements in law school sealed his fate.

While campaigning for the GOP nomination against President Nixon in the 1972 primary, California representative Pete McCloskey was asked at a press conference in his state headquarters across the street from the state capitol whether he would be willing if nominated to select then Massachusetts senator Edward Brooke to be his running mate.

McCloskey not only said that that would be a proposition

which would be agreeable to him but that if the ticket were turned around and Brooke was the nominee and he was the running mate, that would be just as dandy.

Afterward I asked McCloskey's New Hampshire campaign manager, Michael Brewer, what he had thought of McCloskey's response to the query. Brewer let me know that the candidate we were both working for lacked a filter in his mind that virtually every seeker of major office in this land has installed sooner or later. Such a device permits a candidate to appear to the press and public to be spontaneous and frank when he really isn't.

McCloskey and Biden share this trait, which makes them interesting subjects to cover in a campaign, but not so for those laboring away on their campaigns.

In the history of the primary only six men—Dwight Eisenhower and Estes Kefauver in 1952, Gerald Ford in 1976, Gary Hart in 1984, Paul Tsongas in 1992 and John McCain in 2000—managed to not only win their first (contested) New Hampshire presidential primary, but also had managed to avoid any defeat in politics prior to their primary win.

This was a rather easy standard for Eisenhower to meet for, after all, the '52 primary was the first time in his life that he'd ever faced the voters.

The sudden arrival of the other five on the national scene meant the national press corps was confronted with the chore of learning as much as they could as the campaign shifted to the tarmac-to-tarmac phase.

It also provided the press and political leadership a chance to see whether the candidate who'd won in the first vote had the ability to find and attract the talent to his national staff to begin to construct a national campaign.

Not everyone can pass this test, for despite winning four primaries and five caucuses by March 19, 1992, Paul Tsongas withdrew from the race, primarily due to exhaustion. It was unusual that during the final week of that year's New Hampshire primary Tsongas took a day off to rest at his home in Lowell, just across the border from New Hampshire. This is something that is quite rare in a nomination struggle and certainly that Bill Clinton did not do.

Whatever the future for the system of nominating presidential candidates, it is doubtful that any replacement would include one of the most critical components of what currently takes place in the first primary.

The most crucial part of building an organizational structure is the kaffeeklatsch. Given the small size of the state it is possible with several dozen such events, particularly in the four southern and eastern counties where 73.3% of the population now resides (as compared to 64% in the 1950 census), that if a candidate can make a strong enough impression he will find he has secured a toehold.

Without being able to accomplish this it is quite difficult for any hopeful to advance to the next stage—having several hundred supporters reaching out via the telephone, mailings, door-to-door leafleting and canvassing, and also rallies—which enables a candidate to catch fire in the final weeks. That all becomes possible only when a candidate is able to turn up his stumping to a level his opponents can't maintain.

But it all begins with the kaffeeklatsch. It is here where the foundation is laid.

Over a period of more than a decade in the city of Concord the salon of choice for many a Democratic hopeful to audition before a group of activists and observers was the home of Mary Louise Hancock, who resides on the aptly named Washington Street.

Robert Nardini wrote in the February 1988 issue of *Yankee* magazine,

If the New Hampshire primary were a Monopoly game, the square marked GO, for Democrats, would be Mary Louise [Hancock]'s living room. As capital of the state, Concord is the capital of the primary, too. Candidates prefer to be photographed in picturesque villages, and more votes are to be had in larger cities like Manchester and Nashua. But it all begins in this city of 32,000 people who can comparison-shop two or three candidates, if they wish, while downtown on weekly errands.

Hancock served as director of the office of State Planning from 1960 to 1976 and as a state senator from 1976 to 1979. She now spends a good part of the year on the shores of the Bay of Fundy at her second home on picturesque Deer Island, New Brunswick, Canada, but there was a time when just about every Democratic hopeful showed up at her Concord home.

One such politician was the governor of Arkansas, Bill Clinton, who appeared in late April 1987. In the end Clinton decided not to run in 1988 but he managed to do so and win four years later.

Attending such a conclave a day following Clinton's speech to the Democratic State Committee in the millyard in Manchester, I was struck by how much more personable and less programmatic Clinton was in front of the group of only about a dozen folks than he had been the day before.

The session lasted more than an hour and what was so striking was how knowledgeable Clinton was, not simply on state of Arkansas issues and his policies there, but also about national matters and how the game of politics worked.

In listening to him talk I was reminded of Bill Dunfey, a longtime Democratic leader (he died in February 1991), who used to talk about John Kennedy's incredible knowledge of each state. Dunfey served as campaign coordinator for the three northern

New England states in the general election in 1960. Kennedy lost all three but it certainly had more to do with the region's residual anti-Catholicism than the effort that Dunfey and others made on Kennedy's behalf.

It was also similar to hearing Bob Dole explain what it was like to campaign with Richard Nixon and gain the same impression of his complete grasp of what each state was like. This perhaps explains why the Kennedy–Nixon battle in 1960 was so close.

After Clinton finished speaking at Hancock's home he stood up and the two of us started to converse. I told the governor he'd given an impressive performance, as had Gary Hart, who a few months before had also spoken at Hancock's.

I remember Clinton's remarking that he felt he wasn't going to have to worry about having Hart as an opponent if he ran for the presidency.

The fact that within a few days the Donna Rice scandal surfaced showed that Clinton had a good pipeline into what was happening behind the scenes.

About six weeks after Clinton's appearance at the Hancock residence Tennessee senator Albert Gore conducted a similar low-key event. I had asked Clinton if he knew Gore and he remarked that he really didn't know Gore very well, certainly something that changed once he selected him as his running mate on July 9, 1992, just before the opening of the Democratic National Convention in New York City on July 13.

On Saturday, Feb. 8, 1992, Nebraska senator Bob Kerrey spoke to an audience at the Franklin Pierce Law Center in Concord. On his campaign flyers the senator used the slogan "When you see a leader, you know it."

In attempting to convince the electorate of your leadership abilities it usually doesn't hurt to at least trot out your resume in some form. In addition, you don't need a doctorate in political science to figure out that Americans seem to have a proclivity toward electing governors—not senators or members of the U.S. House—to the presidency.

During Kerrey's address and the questions that followed he failed to mention anything about his experiences as governor of the Cornhusker State from 1983 to 1987. Surely you'd think there would be one thing he'd done as the chief executive of his native state that would assist him in making the sale to the voters in the premier primary—yet he failed to mention it. No anecdote, humorous recollection, mention of a success or stumble as governor, nor any musings or reflections on his actions while in the capitol in Lincoln with this nation's only unicameral legislature—all were missing that day at the law school.

The Nebraska senator finished third in that primary, trailing Tsongas and Clinton with just 11% of the vote. By March 5, after winning just the South Dakota primary on Feb. 25, Kerrey dropped out of the race.

During the same primary campaign Hillary Clinton spoke at the same law school. Virtually all of her remarks were about her husband's long service as governor of Arkansas, a post he'd initially won in 1978 only to lose his reelection bid in 1980; he'd won the office back in 1982 and held onto it until he won the White House in November 1992.

Just prior to the 1996 GOP primary I talked with Ralph Jimenez, a reporter from the *Boston Globe* who is now the editorial page editor of the *Concord Monitor*, about the candidate he was covering, Indiana's senator Richard Lugar, who finished fifth with just 5% of the GOP vote.

During the conversation I ran off a list of Midwestern candidates who'd failed here—starting with Robert Taft in 1952—and said that there seems to be a well-established pattern of defeat for candidates from that region.

Jimenez acknowledged the point when he started to discuss Lugar's inability to register much in the way of facial expressions. As we continued to talk it seemed more and more obvious that a part of this country that is known for its flat topography appears to have produced (albeit with a few exceptions) several generations of would-be presidents with equally flat personalities.

This is a circumstance that may not bode well for any future Midwestern challengers for the Oval Office, for with the increased emphasis on television style and demeanor, candidates lacking in some combination charm, warmth and an ability to emote (a lack Bill Clinton was never accused of having) are at a distinct disadvantage.

Much of the reason for the establishment of Super Tuesday in 1988 was to try to alleviate the complaint from the South that its Democratic candidates a quadrennium before—Sen. Ernest Hollings of South Carolina and Askew of Florida—weren't given a fair shake.

Yet if there's a region of the nation that has a complaint with New Hampshire's inordinate amount of influence it would be the Midwest—the seven states of Ohio, Indiana, Illinois, Iowa, Nebraska, Kansas and Missouri.

Since 1952, 15 times candidates from this region have failed to win the first primary. Five times candidates from the Midwest have placed second in the Granite State, an equal number have placed third and two each have placed fourth and fifth. Bob Dole holds the record for a Midwestern candidate for the poorest performance, finishing eighth in the 1980 GOP primary, with 597 votes—just 0.4%. And this was just four years after running for vice president on a ticket headed by President Gerald Ford.

One factor in this poor performance from the heartland of America is the fact that no governor there has ever competed in the New Hampshire primary, leaving out the job that the public seems to gravitate to more than any other.

The reality that so many campaigners from this region have lost so often says something about the ability of Southern types such as Kefauver, Carter and Clinton to charm voters; it also says something about the ability of regional favorite sons—John Kennedy, Lodge, Dukakis and Tsongas—to use geography to their advantage.

Much of the race for the presidency, even in the first primary state, takes place on stage—and a televised one at that. Not all Midwestern candidates come across as lifeless automatons; Indiana senator Birch Bayh raised the roof at the Wayfarer Convention Center at the Democratic State Convention with his keynote address in 1970. But more often than not hopefuls from the Midwest have exhibited all the pizzazz of Paul Simon of Illinois, who will never be compared to John Kennedy, Ronald Reagan or Bill Clinton in his ability to electrify a crowd.

(Although Dwight Eisenhower was born in Texas and raised in Kansas and Ronald Reagan was a product of Illinois, it had been many decades since each had lived in the heartland of this nation and therefore they could not be considered Midwesterners by the time they ascended to the presidency.)

This analysis of regionalism does not mean to suggest that Midwestern aspirants have turned out to be the only personality-free hopefuls—witness Steve Forbes and Missouri-born Bill Bradley—both residents of New Jersey: Neither will ever have to fear being elected to the campaigners' or public speakers' hall of fame.

It appears that having a personality does help in one's travels on the road to the White House. And increasingly it does not hinder a campaign if while under attack a candidate has the ability to reveal some emotion and some fight, as long as it's carried out in a dignified fashion, not on a flatbed truck in front of the *Union Leader*.

The Hawkeye and Granite states happen to be the two locations where the electorate has its chance to size the candidates up in forums other than television. Any change to a format that increases the voter pool would mean the end of the ability of voters in these two states (or any other state, for that matter) to see in person what kind of human being aspires to lead this land.

When the initial New Hampshire primary was held in 1916 it was not the first-in-the-nation primary. That honor went to Indiana, which voted on March 7, a week before New Hampshire. By 1920 Indiana had decided to switch to a later date (May 4) to permit it more time to gain a sense of the nominating campaigns, and thus New Hampshire moved to the first spot by default.

It would no doubt have resulted in many different outcomes if Indiana had not switched to May in 1920, and instead had remained first all this time. Surely it would have made it easier for candidates from the Midwest to gain a toehold, but given the changing nature of campaigns and the strong pull toward TV as the main medium to communicate with the electorate, it is doubtful that if Indiana were still first there would have been a President Hartke, Simon, Harkin or Lugar.

It is unfortunate that with the hundreds of television stations spread across this land, so little emerges from this medium from the brief reports that now pass for coverage of those who wish to lead this nation.

However, the old stand-by—the newspaper—does from time to time offer some useful clues about those running for president, especially in the initial primary state.

Following the 1988 primary the *Concord Monitor* noted in an editorial,

> We learned much about Sen. Robert Dole, for example, when in conversation, he couldn't name a single book that had influenced him nor, without prompting, a movie that he'd

seen in modern times. A slight matter, but one that spoke loudly when combined with Dole's inability to present a vision of what he sought for America. Voters learned from his deportment in defeat—"Stop lying about my record," he snarled to Bush—that the famous Dole temper had only been dormant, not conquered.

Knowing what Bill Bradley has been reading in the way of books should never be the reason for someone to decide whether to vote for the former senator from New Jersey. Yet Bradley's refusal to let the public know during the last campaign reveals an individual who gives a whole new meaning to the expression "button-down." And declining to discuss what he's recently read often leaves the media with one simple question: If he can't talk about his life, why should anyone care what that life is?

Jon Keller is a reporter for Channel 56 in Boston, primarily known for his offbeat and iconoclastic treatment of politicians and public issues.

Keller was the reporter who bellowed out to Lamar Alexander at the conclusion of a rally on the Milford Oval just before the 1996 primary asking whether he happened to know the cost of a quart of milk and a dozen eggs. Instead of admitting that he had no clue what each cost, Alexander turned to an aide and ordered, "I need you to find out the price of milk and eggs—right now."

Although Keller was the recipient of some negative reaction from some members of the press, he was attempting to prove the point that the former governor (1979 to 1987) of Tennessee was a faux populist and not the real McCoy.

Alexander had come from far back in the pack to emerge in the final week of the 1996 primary with a chance of pulling off a patented New Hampshire primary upset. (If he had done so he could have generated one of the more interesting headlines in the history of the primary: "The Tennessee Walker wins.")

But, alas, it turned out that the man dressed in plaid was the sum of his consultants' advice, not unlike Joe Biden, for *Newsweek* had revealed that his everyman's outfit had been the idea of a consultant in 1977 to show how much of a commoner he really was.

(What is it about Tennessee that it can move in half a century from Estes Kefauver's coonskin cap to Alexander's plaid man walking 100 miles across the Granite State? Maybe if Al Gore had devised a similar gimmick he would at least have carried his own home state—instead, he was the first nominee since George McGovern who failed to win his own home state. If he had won Tennessee he would have become the president.)

After losing in the general election for governor in 1974 Alexander managed to win the post four years later. He achieved this after a five-month, 1,000-mile walking tour of the Volunteer State—while wearing his soon-to-be-famous red-and-black plaid flannel shirt.

One of the ways to research the backgrounds of the various presidential contenders is to use the monthly publication *Current Biography*.

The one from July 1991 on Alexander, who had served as the secretary of education under President George H. W. Bush from 1991 to 1993, details a rather impressive biography, maybe strong enough to help him win the White House. Yet as the nation learned in 1996 and 2000 a strong resume does not make for a strong candidate, at least in the case of Lamar Alexander.

When he announced his candidacy in his hometown of Maryville (pop. 19,208) in the Great Smoky Mountains on Feb. 28, 1995, he was once again wearing his now standard-issue red-and-black plaid shirt, strolling along parts of his paper route from his youth. Alexander was lacking in the combination of manners and common sense to at least dress appropriately for the occasion.

The outfit could lead one to conclude that the gimmick had outgrown the man who tried to use it and he had to prove even on the notable day he threw his hat into the ring that he was easily the most fashion-challenged of all the presidential hopefuls. Such a down-home technique seemed to affirm that this was yet another campaign "of the consultants, by the consultants and for the consultants."

Without any doubt the sizable sum of money the presidential wannabes poured into WMUR-TV in Manchester in 1996 and 2000 are the clearest indications of how much more like the rest of the country this state has become.

Steve Forbes's shelling out $848,000 of the $2.6 million the GOP spent on this one station in 1996 is the most obvious demonstration of how grassroots and person-to-person campaigning is in jeopardy in the primary primary. But is it? The winner of that primary—commentator Pat Buchanan by 2,136 votes over Bob Dole—spent only $232,000 and he delayed his ad buys on this station until Jan. 29, just 23 days before the vote on Feb. 20.

If Forbes had emerged victorious in 1996 (he finished fourth) or in 2000 (third place) the national media would have gleefully pointed out that New Hampshire's tradition of one-on-one stumping was history. But John McCain's victory in 2000 and the use of 114 town meetings was additional evidence to the skeptics that the state was not for sale. Still, WMUR managed to come away another winner with receipts of about $3 million between 1999 and the vote on Feb. 1, 2000.

Even with their drawbacks there is something timeless not only about the first primary state but also the first caucus state. To use a sports comparison, they seem comparable to Fenway Park in Boston and Wrigley Field in Chicago. Both ballparks are antiques that somehow still work in spite of a mediocre team in the Midwest and one in New England that has been unable to win the deciding game of a World Series since 1918.

Obviously the biggest winner in the last primary was WMUR, for it was announced in September 2000 that Hearst-Argyle Inc., the owner or manager of 29 TV stations and a few radio stations, had purchased the Manchester station for $185 million. The sale was completed on March 28, 2001.

Channel 9 was this state's first television operation; its initial broadcast from 1819 Elm Street aired on March 26, 1954. Its founding owner was Francis Murphy, who was the state's first Catholic governor and a Republican elected in 1936 and reelected versus John L. Sullivan by 26,994 votes in 1938. (Sullivan had lost to Styles Bridges in the controversial election for governor in 1934. By 1942 Murphy had switched parties and in that year he lost to Bridges in the U.S. Senate race by 14,945 votes.)

Francis Murphy died on Dec. 19, 1958, and within a few weeks the station was sold by his estate to United Broadcasting Co. In 1981 TV 9 was sold to Imes Communication (based in Columbus, Mississippi), the owner until the sale in 2000. Manchester is this nation's 64th largest TV market.

President Bill Clinton was interviewed by WMUR in the Old Executive Office Building on Feb. 7, 1995, roughly a year away from the 1996 primary. Reflecting on the state's role, the president stated,

> I just—I always believed in the New Hampshire primary process as an observer. But after I went through it, I felt more strongly about it, because I don't think you could go there and be with those folks without being profoundly moved by the human dimension of public life and the enormous responsibilities we have here. . . . But the truth is that the people there are intensely public-minded and know a phenomenal amount about the issues, and they're fair-minded.
>
> And, you know, I have—again it's only based on my experience and the lifetime of friendships I made there, but I feel very strongly about it. I think it works.

In *The New Yorker* Hendrik Hertzberg wrote just before the last primary,

> I've been visiting New Hampshire during primary season ever since 1968, and what struck me this time was how familiar the basic rituals seemed, given the convulsive changes in politics—the big money, the eclipse of volunteer activism, the media craziness, the direct-mail revolution, the polling explosion. It all still happens, event to event, on a human scale—in hotel function rooms, on sidewalks, at civic clubs. It's still amazingly easy to see candidates, even meet them and ask them questions. On one recent two-and-a-half-day foray, I had no trouble catching a Bill Bradley rally at a Lions Club in Hudson, a George W. Bush speech and press conference at Manchester West High School, and a couple of John McCain "town meetings," in a Holiday Inn in Dover and a middle-school gym in Candia, with enough time left over to attend two all-candidate debates and have a late drink at the Wayfarer.

Any review of the countless articles written and aired since the primary arrived on the national scene just over a half-century ago points up the virtual absence of reports that explore the angle of a favorite-son candidacy here. Few exist.

There was some speculation (almost two-thirds of a page in the May 4, 1962, issue of *Time*) that examined Governor Wesley Powell's presidential aspirations and some coverage in 1999 of Sen. Bob Smith's brief and utterly unsuccessful attempt to make headway as he sought the GOP nomination before leaving the party for a short time.

The state has been hammered by writers such as Neal Peirce for the absence of "great leaders," but is this not an asset instead of a liability?

In the half-century of presidential primaries since the names of the candidates were placed on the ballot alongside those of delegate hopefuls in 1952, the lack of political leadership has guaranteed one of the most important factors this small state brings to the table in the determination of the fates of the presidential aspirants: Every quadrennium New Hampshire has served as a level playing field in this nation of ours.

Can one imagine how tilted the playing field would be if one of the four largest states—California, Texas, New York or Florida—held the first primary instead? How much more difficult would it be for candidates from other states to get any sort of hearing or secure a toehold in order to make their case if confronted with trying to woo millions of voters far more familiar with their own governor or senators if one or more of them decides to seek the presidency?

Just how level a playing field the Granite State offers was put to a test prior to the 2000 primary. For the first time in the history of the modern primary (since 1952) there was actually an individual holding major office here—senior senator Bob Smith—who announced his candidacy for the GOP nod. He did this in the same high school—Kingswood Regional High School in Wolfeboro—where he had taught from 1970 to 1973. From 1975 to 1985 he had been a realtor in Wolfeboro, and he was elected to the First District congressional seat in 1984 after unsuccessful bids in 1980 and 1982.

Smith first won election to the Senate in 1990, replacing two-term fellow Republican Gordon Humphrey, who stood by his pledge to serve just two terms.

Even after he narrowly won reelection against former Second District congressman Democrat Dick Swett by just 14,907 votes, not all considered Smith much in the way of presidential timber despite his height (6′6″, placing him in Mo Udall territory as far as height went for a would-be president).

Once upon a time there was a columnist for the *Boston Globe* named Andrew Merton, who still teaches English at the University of New Hampshire in Durham. He regarded Smith's presidential aspirations as a threat to the primary, just as Democratic senator Tom Harkin's bid in 1992 closed down the Iowa event to all other challengers.

In his Jan. 2, 1993 column, after analyzing the fact that the state had lost its bellwether status in 1992 with Clinton's eventual victory after losing here (Clinton just happens to be Smith's middle name), Merton opined, "True, we can still say: No *Republican* [italics his] has won the presidency without winning the New Hampshire primary first. A thin reed to cling to, but there it is." The column continued,

> Smith could crush that reed like a boulder rolling down Mount Washington. For if he runs for president, he will win New Hampshire's Republican primary.
>
> He will win, not because he is best qualified to be president even among the likely Republican candidates; he will win because nobody else will play.

After a review of recent political history Merton came to this conclusion: "If Smith runs, those non-Iowa Caucus stories of 1992 will become non-New Hampshire primary stories of 1996. If President Clinton runs for reelection, the Democratic primary will not be competitive. And with Smith in and everyone else out, the Republican primary will be meaningless."

In the next to last paragraph the writer added just for good measure: "For in his heart Bob Smith must know that the New Hampshire primary does not provide a fair opening for the presidential primary season. And he knows that if he runs in '96, he will forever destroy the mystique of the first-in-the-nation primary."

Smith did not run in '96; he waited until 1999. But all the TV station owners, hotel and restaurant operators, car rental locations, printers, phone companies and office space landlords did not have to worry about Bob Smith's chasing away all the other GOP contenders as Iowan Tom Harkin did to the Democratic field in 1992.

The year of his race for the nomination turned out to be a rather strange odyssey for our senior senator until his defeat in the September 2002 GOP primary, for on July 13, 1999, he gave a speech on the floor of the Senate in which he announced his decision to leave the Grand Old Party; he also attacked the influence of consultants.

But he promised to continue his presidential aspirations as an independent and considered accepting the nomination of the U.S. Taxpayers Party, which changed its name to the Constitution Party. He decided not to run under this banner after discovering that some of the membership of this group was anti-Catholic.

Smith, lagging badly in the polls and his fundraising efforts proving to be equally lackluster, finally announced on Oct. 28 that he was leaving the presidential race; he also returned to the GOP.

Although Smith was an active candidate, any objective observer would have a difficult, if not impossible, task to find any evidence that his bid created even a moment's hesitation for any other contender in the nation's first primary.

If this isn't evidence that the first primary has always been and continues to be as level a playing field as one can find among the 50 states, I don't know what is.

After all, Bob Smith had about as much of a chance to win the nomination in 1996 or 2000 as former Ohio representative James Traficant had to be selected *Time* magazine's Person of the Year in 2002.

Asked his opinion of the presidential prospects of this state's top political leaders, Martin Gross said, "We know our officeholders well enough to know that we don't want them to be president." He added, "We're not going to be dominated by favorite son or favorite daughterism here."

There have been just a few minor exceptions to the level playing field concept for the "quadrennial coldwater fiesta to hook the tourist dollar."

By law the names of candidates and also delegates (which were removed from the ballots by the 1980 primary) are supposed to be rotated so that a candidate whose name starts with Z has as much of a chance of being on the top of the ballot as someone whose name starts with A.

That was not the case in 1952 when Sen. Bob Taft of Ohio was locked in a tough fight for the GOP nomination with Dwight Eisenhower.

It just so happens that when the ballots were printed the Taft camp cried foul when it was discovered that while the names for the 14 delegate positions were rotated, the four names listed in the so-called beauty contest were not. Hence Taft's name would be listed last on every ballot, trailing Eisenhower, former Minnesota governor Harold Stassen and even an unknown attorney from St. Louis by the name of William Schneider.

The state attorney general at the time was Gordon Tiffany, who had been legislative counsel to Gov. Sherman Adams, prior to being appointed attorney general in 1950.

Tiffany ruled that since the presidential preference poll was advisory in nature the law requiring the rotation of names was not valid. Because most of the 350,000 ballots had been sent to the polling places, Taft decided not to take legal action.

(On Nov. 29, 1989, Tiffany was interviewed at a retirement home in Concord for a documentary on Sherman Adams. He was asked about this controversy but he had no recollection of what had transpired 37 years earlier.)

The next case of a tilted playing field was in 1980. When I first heard about the plan to have a debate just between George H. W. Bush and Ronald Reagan in Nashua sponsored by the *Nashua Telegraph* the Saturday prior to the Feb. 26 primary, I simply could not believe such an inane idea would be carried out.

If there were ever an example of how not to conduct a debate during a first primary, this was it.

Agreeing to limit participation to just these two men (a determination that was made after just one state—Iowa, with its Jan. 21 caucus—had been heard from) meant that five men who also sought the GOP nomination would be silenced. If these five men were the political equivalent of chopped liver, the logic of this exclusionary policy would have been understandable.

However, by denying access to one of the world's great microphones to these individuals, Jon Breen, editor of the *Nashua Telegraph* and the moderator for the evening's festivities, managed to give the heave-ho to some fairly accomplished political acts.

One was Bob Dole, who was thought highly enough of to be picked as President Gerald Ford's running mate in the previous presidential election and who had served as a senator from Kansas since 1969. Another was Howard Baker of Tennessee, a senator since 1966. Two congressmen from Illinois were also kicked off the stage that wild night in Nashua: John Anderson (since 1960) and Phil Crane (since 1969). And, although he did not show, no doubt he would also have been refused admittance—the former governor of Texas (from 1963 to 1969) and the secretary of the Treasury in the Nixon administration from 1971 to 1972—John Connally.

In the 1980 primary there was a lot less preening for the TV cameras than there has been since, but there were still moments of a true Hollywood "character" that the characters in this state had to endure.

The town of Hopkinton, population 5,399, just to the west of the state capital, has as picturesque a town center as one can find in all of New England.

Incorporated in 1765, it has a town hall that is a frequent stopping place in elections, presidential primary and otherwise.

A few months before the GOP primary on Feb. 26, 1980, former California governor Ronald Reagan gave a speech in the

Hopkinton Town Hall. It wasn't a stirring or memorable oration, but the former actor surely had a stage presence and he could connect with an audience, particularly when he could get off a one-liner that called Sen. Ted Kennedy's plan for national health care simply "Teddy care."

After he finished his speech he and his wife, Nancy, headed for the front door of the hall and walked alongside a wooden barricade to shake some hands and then proceed to the campaign bus.

Standing behind the barricade was a mother with her daughter, who looked about 16 years of age. The daughter was holding a book that contained her prized collection of autographs. She was in prime position to secure one from someone who would be the 40th president of the United States in just over a year.

It was interesting to watch the interplay between these two as Reagan moved closer to where they stood. But instead of stopping for all of four or five seconds to add his name to this girl's prized collection of autographs, he slipped her a business card with a facsimile of his signature.

The crestfallen look on her face was something to watch as she fell back a bit into the embrace of her mother, who needed to shore up her very disappointed daughter, both physically and psychologically.

Such a display of Hollywood sincerity in the end did not cost Reagan the election no matter how many printed business cards he managed to pass out during that primary. After all, he did win the GOP battle by 27%, the third highest winning margin in a contested race—topped only by Richard Nixon's 47.8% win in 1972 and the 66.8% Nixon secured in 1968 against the write-in for Nelson Rockefeller, after George Romney withdrew from the race on Feb. 28.

As this is being written, just about a year from the next New Hampshire primary (which is scheduled for Jan. 27, 2004, the first time the primary will be held in that month of the year), you can be sure about one thing that will not happen.

It is highly unlikely that the former Democratic governor of Vermont, Howard Dean, will be whipping out any business cards already printed with his signature instead of taking a few seconds to sign an autograph for those he meets and greets in the Granite State in his bid for the presidency.

On Friday, Dec. 3, 1999, the *Union Leader* made known its selection for the GOP primary. "George Bush has said virtually nothing substantial in this campaign because he thinks it will get him the nomination. And John McCain will say virtually anything because he thinks it will get him attention."

In addition, publisher Joseph McQuaid's front-page editorial above the fold noted,

> Bush is a nice guy but an empty suit with no philosophical underpinning.
>
> McCain would finish a strong second, in the Democrat's race.
>
> Steven Forbes is not charismatic. (Some would say he looks like a geek.) But he's also not a phony. Ask him a question, you'll get a thoughtful answer, not a soundbite.

The editorial then mentioned in its last paragraph that Forbes "is one tough, smart customer who can be the strong, principled leader America needs."

But, alas, once again "the paper," as it is often referred to north of Boston, failed to show up in the winner's circle. That was an honor granted to Senator McCain. In the final seven polls released the day before the vote, just one predicted a Bush victory. The American Research Group had the governor of Texas ahead by two percentage points over McCain. This group's daily tracking poll had Bush moving ahead of the Arizona senator on the final Friday before the Tuesday tally. On Sunday ARG had the next president in the lead by five points. McCain won by 18.

John McCain's landslide victory proved that Iowa is in no way, shape or form the determining factor in the outcome of any first-in-the-nation primary. If the Republican (and Independent) voters here had ratified the Iowa choice (George W. Bush) the race would have been over.

The Democratic result with Gore winning in both states might have proven different if the final round of polling here had proven to be more accurate, for clearly Bill Bradley could have used the Independents' trying to find a way to get the most value from their ballots. This group went for McCain in droves, costing Bradley his chance to win a squeaker here; instead, he lost by just 6,395 votes.

Another way of assessing what happened is to argue that once again the concept of strategic or survival voting took place. This idea contends that when the voter enters the polling booth that voter does not pick the next president, but makes a judgment as to which candidate can make the best use of his or her vote. In a place that is as frugal as the Granite State, not striving for the best possible use of a person's vote could only be considered aberrational behavior.

As has been said before, the role the first primary plays is not to elect the next president, nor even to nominate, but to elevate onto the national stage individuals almost every quadrennium.

In 2000, the state of Delaware persisted with its GOP primary four days later in violation of the New Hampshire–decreed seven-day halo, but only Steve Forbes campaigned there. Once again he won as he had a quadrennium before; both times he also carried Arizona. Therefore, one can now say that as Delaware goes, so goes Arizona.

Bush's campaign effort here could only be described as lackadaisical, but since his was a national campaign and not the very targeted approach that McCain had to pursue, he had the luxury of taking a hit and then moving on down the road—something no one else in the Republican field could manage.

The Straight Talk Express pulled up in front of the state capitol around noontime on the day before the 2000 primary. John McCain and his wife, Cindy, detrained from the now-famous bus and soon were strolling up Park Street, where the senator would speak to a crowd of about 250 on the State House plaza. About half the crowd was made up of reporters and their support troops.

As the McCains started to walk up the street, trailing behind them was former senator Warren Rudman. Among the crowd lining the sidewalk was Tom Brokaw, the anchorman for the NBC Evening News. He greeted the former senator, who was one of the few prominent GOP leaders to back McCain, but Rudman did not acknowledge him. The problem was that Brokaw was not wearing a suit but a parka and denim jeans. Rudman belatedly recognized Brokaw and told him that the reason he had failed to acknowledge his greeting was that he had not recognized him because he was dressed like one of the locals.

Also trailing behind the candidate and his wife were two of their children, who, since a snowstorm had just ended, started to throw snowballs at each other.

Obviously not all the energy that day was connected with the weather, but so much snow made a nifty background for the speech of the soon-to-be-victorious GOP hopeful. Although not a mob scene, it was quite an event that final day before the voters trekked to the polls.

McCain, who very early in the process jettisoned the concept of delivering prepared remarks, was more like a talking tape recorder: His comments were familiar since he'd made them so often along the campaign trail.

However, from the response of the crowd that seemed to be the last thing on their minds, for clearly the Granite State was getting ready for yet another patented upset. By rejecting the winner in Iowa (Bush) the voters here were preparing once again to empower the states down the road, for obviously, if McCain lost here he couldn't (as proved to be the case with Bill Bradley) win anywhere.

Perhaps the writer who best captured the contrasting campaign style of Governor Bush in the waning hours here was Mary
McGrory of the *Washington Post*, who wrote,

> New Hampshire voters were also unimpressed when
> George W., the day before the election, went into a veritable
> decathlon of frivolities—he snowmobiled, waltzed, and
> flipped pancakes. It was a beguiling show of energy, but New
> Hampshire takes its first primary responsibilities seriously.
> George Bush didn't until the astonishing "bump in the road"
> John McCain's 18-point lead—smote him.

Martin Gross said,

> In the final analysis the New Hampshire advantage when
> it comes to the presidential primary is a way to demonstrate
> that [a] candidate can gain a relationship with voters in an
> effective way and not necessarily only through the mass
> media. . . . I've always thought the perpetuation of the New
> Hampshire primary is a strange circular motion: Candidates
> wanting to come here and the press agreeing to come here to
> follow them. If you take either of them away the New
> Hampshire primary is done for.

Reflecting on what happened in the last first primary Gross
stated,

> John McCain did well in the New Hampshire primary in
> 2000 because I think people were responding to what they per-
> ceive as [a] good moral compass and an attention to what the
> candidate believed was right. I believe what happened here in
> the 2000 primary to me was a celebration of the insight of the
> New Hampshire voters.
> Regardless of the blandishments of corporate America

New Hampshire voters were not persuaded that George W. Bush was the genuine article.

Gross supported Al Gore for president not just in 2000 but in his disorganized and lackluster bid in 1988. Of his defeat here, Gross opined,

> When voters don't see a substantial difference between the candidates they tend to vote Republican and where they can't relate to a Democratic candidate they don't vote for him. I don't think New Hampshire voters related to Al Gore. I'm sorry, Al Gore is a fine man but Al Gore could not get people to relate to him. In my own case even after 14 years of knowing him and knowing about him I still don't know who he is.

As a fundraising instrument for the office of the New Hampshire secretary of state the last primary generated the least revenue from the $1,000 required to place a name in the presidential contest since 1984.

In 1983 a revision in the law dropped the provision that 500 signatures from each of the two congressional districts was necessary. That same revision doubled the filing fee from $500.

Only 30 presidential wannabes filed last time, far below the 61 in 1992 and also trailing the 43 in 1996 and 37 in 1988. It did exceed the 27 candidates listed in 1984. Still, the $198,000 collected since 1984 isn't chump change.

The turnout in 2000, in the words of Secretary of State William Gardner (who accurately predicted a record vote) turned out to be "a record record." Gardner predicted that 191,000 would participate in the GOP primary; it was actually 238,606. He estimated that the Democratic vote would be 60,000; it turned out to be 154,639. Overall the vote was almost 45,000 more than the previous record set in 1992.

In an editorial the day after the decision the *Boston Globe* wrote,

> New Hampshire's voice commands attention for one reason above all others: The state speaks well because it listens well. . . . But the crucial point is that these people know what they're doing. They know how to question and make judgments about the candidates individually, while not being overly impressed with big spending or establishment backing. . . .
>
> The biggest winner yesterday was the New Hampshire primary itself, which proved once again that it performs well as the nation's ear.
>
> New Hampshire deserves to be first.

One of the drawbacks to the way the primary is now conducted is how little time the hopefuls devote to the northern part of the state—the land often referred to as being north of the notches.

The day following the last primary the *Boston Globe* displayed maps of where the top five candidates traveled after the Iowa caucus on Jan. 24. Only Bill Bradley and Steve Forbes managed to wander north of the notches during that last week and all the rest of the campaign activity took place essentially in the southern tier.

This is understandable since so much of the population now lives in the southern tier, but now candidates are tied to the local TV stations and to satellite dishes as much as contenders of yesteryear were attached to political bosses. It is quite unlikely that a similar tracking of where candidates are scheduled in the final week of the 2004 race will be any different.

In the novel *The Wisest Man in America*, published by the University Press of New England in 1995, author W. D. Wetherell created the lead character, Ferris, with a record of always predicting the winner of each presidential primary.

Wetherell, who has lived in the Upper Valley town of Lyme for more than two decades, refers to his adopted state as being the "crankiest state in the union." And just as in real life, candidates manage to flood into the state—but in this novel they are referred to, at one point, as the "presidentialites." These candidates manage to "learn to disguise what's inside."

Ferris, a logger, happens to reside in one of the notches; in describing the location he says, "We're so high that anything falling hits us first." It is a place where life as it used to be still is.

In contrast, the bottom tier of the state does not draw much in the way of praise from Ferris:

> But it will get busy again, the tax evaders and the easy money men will move north from Massachusetts just the way they've moved north ever since this state began. I hardly know what to make of that whole lower third, it's changed so much from when I was younger. Changed, so even from high up it's all a blur of ugliness and confusion and noise, and even if I go higher, try looking down on it the way I did those other places, it's still a blur and a fog and a great lookalike nothing that extends, I'm told, all the way to Florida.

IV

THE ALTERNATIVE IS?

"I'm counting the minutes until the New Hampshire primary so we can get past the grotesque obsession with the media-coddled citizens of that marginal state," seethed social critic Camille Paglia. "New Hampshire's tyranny over national politics must end."
— Faye Fiore, www.latimes.com/newsnation, Jan. 26, 2000

EARLY IN THE FALL OF 1968, after leaving college the previous spring, I traveled through the Pacific Northwest and then settled in northern California for several months.

After enduring a period of monsoon-like weather living in Marin County, just to the north of San Francisco, I moved to Tucson, Arizona, arriving on Christmas Eve. I found a job as a carpenter's helper and after about a month took a couple of days off to travel by bus to Globe, a town of 6,000 on Highway 60 to the east of Phoenix (and near the community of Tortilla Flat).

This mining town is situated at the eastern edge of the Sierra Ancha mountains and to the south of the Fort Apache Indian Reservation. Globe's basic industry is copper mining and it is named after the Globe mine, a large silver deposit that was discovered in 1873. It is so hardscrabble that it won't ever be confused with places such as Beverly Hills, Bar Harbor or the city I grew up in—Santa Barbara.

Mining is the lifeblood of this town and it certainly has left its mark; when I first visited in 1969 there were mine tailings that seemed to overwhelm everything. (Copper is considered to be the most valuable mineral in the Grand Canyon State.)

It took me about an hour to decide that as different as Globe was, I was better off remaining in Tucson, where I stayed for a couple more months until I traveled east to Connecticut and then to the Granite State.

On leaving Globe for Scottsdale and then Tucson I watched, from the bus on the main street, an individual slowly walking up a steep driveway late in the afternoon to a home that was dilapidated, as much of the housing in Globe was.

What was so unusual about this fellow on that winter day was how covered in dirt he was as he slowly trekked up that steep driveway. It was one of those times when you looked at someone and could reach only one conclusion—this laborer seemed to be carrying the weight of the world on his shoulders. It would not have been hard to guess that he had to toil for a living in Globe's Old Dominion copper mine.

In the campaigns I've worked in (none since 1975) and the ones I've been writing about, I sometimes wonder, as candidates pontificate, whether they have any clue whatsoever about how hard an existence it is not just for that fellow back in Globe, but for millions of other Americans caught up in similar difficult circumstances.

With each passing year it appears that political campaigns are centered around one factor—money—and therefore are less and less closely connected to middle- and lower-income Americans.

Before too many campaign consultants proclaim the era of grassroots organizing over, they should, for the time being, put away their guides to the major TV markets in their megastate manuals and concentrate on the fact that Iowa and New Hampshire still have a requirement that one hopes this nation never loses— the use of good old-fashioned shoe leather to meet and greet as many ordinary citizens with their ordinary lives as possible.

But what is the deeper meaning of this concentration on fundraising—particularly as it relates to the presidential nomination system?

The ability of a Gene McCarthy to spend an estimated $250,000 to almost win the New Hampshire primary in 1968 and then begin to pull together a national effort is no longer in the cards.

Now from the get-go the name of the game is raising money—and who does that leave behind?

It surely doesn't leave the wealthy out of the picture, as everyone found out in 2000 when Texas governor George W. Bush was able to harness awesome fundraising ability from the lists his father had compiled in two decades of running for the presidency—his own lists in Texas and other GOP lists from around the nation. Bush was one of the few who did not need the federal matching system first used in 1976 to finance his campaign for the nomination, although he did use federal funds in the general election.

While all this concentration on raising money increasingly becomes the centerpiece of the race for the White House, what does this change really mean?

If money is changing the nature of our campaigns, it's doubtful that the national press corps has changed much in the three decades that I've been watching New Hampshire presidential primaries.

As they sit around the bar at the Wayfarer and other watering holes discussing the candidates they've been covering, the usual number one topic of interest is no longer William Loeb and his *Manchester Union Leader*.

Now visiting reporters can sit around the same bars (and a few new ones such as the Center of New Hampshire in downtown Manchester) and discuss the candidates they've been covering, but the media fixation has shifted to the contenders with the campaign treasury or personal wealth to ramp up their ad blitzes on the local and regional commercial TV stations.

Because this state was one of the last (if not the last) to

develop a TV component to major state races, the use of television as a campaign weapon has been limited.

That is no longer the case. In 2002 successful businessman Craig Benson shelled out $8.5 million of his own considerable wealth to win the GOP gubernatorial primary by just 4,638 votes over former state senator Bruce Keough. (And former senator Gordon Humphrey finished third, 13,401 votes behind Benson.) Benson then easily won the general election by 21%, or a margin of 90,386 votes against the Democratic nominee, state senator Mark Fernald.

In neighboring Massachusetts in that same election year, wealthy businessman Mitt Romney shelled out $6.1 million from his own pocket to win the governorship.

One of the issues in that campaign was how to attract businesses to the state; Romney was attacked by his Democratic opponent, state treasurer Shannon O'Brien, as someone who was too willing to grant sizable tax breaks to lure businesses.

In the *Boston Globe* on Oct. 1, 2002, reporter Peter Howe quoted Romney, the son of the late governor of Michigan who had sought the presidency in 1968: "I don't stay up at night worrying about the wealthy people. You folks can take care of yourselves. I don't stay up at nights worrying about big businesses. I do worry about small business."

As campaigns become more expensive and more money is directed toward TV ad blitzes, one does wonder what becomes of the voices of those not comfortable enough to be able to afford a contribution of $50 or $100, let alone the $2,000 limit that is now in effect in the race for the White House.

At the end of the day, when middle- and lower-income Americans finish their daily toil, do we still have an electoral process that hears their voices? With fundraising now more and more a factor in each campaign the hope that Jimmy Carter expressed in Nashua on Nov. 6, 1975, seems in greater jeopardy:

I hope that New Hampshire is always the first primary state. I hope that 100 years from now New Hampshire still has the first primary. I think it's good for the country to have at least one relatively small state so that the candidates have to go directly to the voters to shake hands at factory shift lines; go to the high school, the shopping centers, beano games and meet the people where they are.

Once elected, a president faces a significant challenge in trying to run the vast apparatus that constitutes the federal government. With our existing governing system it would be difficult to identify better preparation for that job than to try to pull together a national campaign. The endeavor requires careful organization and the recruitment of capable and energetic managers and administrators. And all the while adroitness, patience, intelligence and stamina must be demonstrated under the klieg lights as reporters and the general populace probe repeatedly to find the strength and substance of the candidate while also searching for flaws and weaknesses.

There's also the need for the candidate to develop that difficult-to-define sixth sense that attempts to pinpoint the complaints, concerns and aspirations of the so-called average American. From that the presidential hopeful must articulate an agenda to address those concerns of the electorate, at the same time inspiring party activists and leaders to organize and try to bring forth victory.

Neither New Hampshire nor Iowa nor any other single primary or caucus state decides who the nominees of the two major parties are. But because of the unique position both these states enjoy they have the power to determine to a great extent who the serious contenders for the Oval Office will be.

With the media notoriety both early states receive, undecided politicians and activists around the country watch their indecision dissolve once the returns are announced from both these states.

The separation of the strong from the weak contenders is accelerated and that harsh process of selection reaches a climax.

The nation's premier primary can be described as the key that may unlock the door that often leads through the complex maze to the nominating convention and then usually to the inaugural ceremony as the president of the United States is sworn into office.

The setting is a TV news director's dream—the snow-covered landscape reminding many across this land where our nation's roots lie; the traditional yet still functioning form of the town meeting; the diversity of the ethnic groups; and the tight-lipped Yankee who reluctantly lets a "country quote" roll off his tongue into the frosty air for any nearby reporter to pull in and embrace like a hot cup of coffee in the north woods.

Every president elected since 1952 has had his start with a first- or second-place finish during the Granite State's "deep frozen inconclusive, misleading carnival of political egotism and pop ideology." This state has propelled obscure pols onto the national stage and helped to drive two presidents (Truman and Johnson) into retirement. All this from a state with just over 1.2 million residents, a total that is exceeded in population by the cities of New York, Los Angeles, Chicago, Boston, Philadelphia and Phoenix.

One of the most significant woes of our ailing nomination process is an infection of the body politic—a condition called *primaryitis*—an ailment that has been spreading for three decades now.

Once the Democratic Party concluded the start of its reform process after the boss-plagued 1968 convention in Chicago there was, according to *Congressional Quarterly*, a sudden jump in the percentage of delegates to both national conventions from just 39.1% in primaries in 1968 to 61% in 1972. It has fallen below that percentage only once since—to 60% in 1984.

In 2000, 70.8% of delegates were picked in the 40 primaries. It is now a system that has left caucuses in the dust and although it is certain that the percentage will never return to the 39% of 1968, it would behoove the party leaders in Washington and around this nation to determine which states are most suitable for conversion back to caucuses.

Obviously any megastate, given the complexity and expense of setting up a caucus in a place with millions of residents, is not a likely candidate for this switch. But there are about a dozen small and medium-sized states that should look at a process that is a far better instrument for strengthening the state and local party structures than the mass-media–dominated primaries.

In March 1968 just one state—New Hampshire—held a primary during that month. By 1972 Florida and Illinois settled on March as well.

In the year 2000 seven states held primaries in the month of February and 21 conducted theirs in March.

What used to be a spread-out series of contests to permit candidates to test themselves and select certain states in which to take a stand and others to bypass for a variety of reasons, has long been a mad dash to gain the earliest possible date on the primary calendar. With each state looking out for itself, this question has been left forgotten: Is this process that has evolved and now changed so dramatically really what's best for this nation? Is this the best system for selecting the best candidates for the White House? Have we found a way that makes for an equilibrium between often competing forces that have a role—in particular, the political leadership and the press and the voting public?

Some are not happy about the system we use to nominate our candidates for president. One is political scientist Thomas Patterson, who has written, "The modern system of picking presidents also places burdens on the candidates that they should not be required to carry. Some of the demands are grotesque. A U.S. presidential campaign requires nearly a two-year stint in the bowels of television studios, motel rooms, and fast-food restaurants."

In the Feb. 28, 1980, issue of the *New York Times*, columnist Anthony Lewis chimed in: "New Hampshire is an utterly unrepresentative state, as we are reminded every four years. It is full of people who think gun control is a Communist plot. It is full of William Loeb. But there is no ignoring the message it sends in our present crazy system of choosing a President."

The *New Republic* published its displeasure on March 7, 1988: "The winner of the first contests—Richard Gephardt in Iowa, Michael Dukakis in New Hampshire—have not in their rhetoric these many months acknowledged the world as it really is. Woe to the Democratic Party if it allows those two idiosyncratic and pampered jurisdictions to circumscribe the nation's choice."

The existing system could also be described as retail here and wholesale just about everywhere else but in Iowa. Given the population of this nation, 281 million (Canada has only 32 million), the movement toward an increasing number of primaries in the past three decades has enhanced our democracy in some ways, but hampered it in others.

A shift back toward more caucuses would not be a cure-all, but it would strengthen the process by involving committed citizens in both major parties and placing the political leadership and grass roots back on a more even footing with the media, fundraisers and the consultant class.

Thomas Patterson, a leading expert on our electoral process, wrote in *The Vanishing Voter*, published by Knopf in 2002,

A stand-alone contest, such as the New Hampshire primary, is the only proven way to reduce the power of money. By campaigning for weeks on end in one state, and pouring every available resource into it (McCain spent $1.5 million in New Hampshire in 2000), a lesser-known candidate can sometimes win and thereby gain the momentum necessary to compete successfully elsewhere. . . .

Frontloading explains why the overall turnout rate in presidential primaries has fallen from nearly 30 to 17 percent since the 1970s. Turnout has become schizophrenic— respectable in states with early contests and embarrassing in those with later contests. . . . Since the advent of frontloading, turnout has been half again as high in contested primaries as in those held after the races were decided. Were it not for the primaries for other offices also being held in the late-scheduled states, almost no one would bother to vote. . . .

The long campaign of today runs in spurts, taxes people's attention, and dulls their sensibilities. . . .

Major moments, such as the New Hampshire primary, Super Tuesday, the conventions, the October debates, and Election Day, have the capacity to engage and inform the public. They are the key to an involved electorate; they bring people into the campaign. . . . But when these moments are widely spread out, their capacity is diminished. Time—in this case, too much time—invites the public to disengage. . . .

A campaign that starts a full year before Election Day may seem to offer everything citizens could possibly want or need. Instead, it sends them forth on a mind-numbing trek. If the election system is to be made fit for the American people, a place to start is the length; shorten it.

It would be easier to reduce the schedules of the 162 games of Major League Baseball and the 16 contests in the National Football League than to shorten the presidential election process.

We should not engage in a fruitless search for a way to condense the primary and caucus calendar, but find a way to add more caucuses and reduce the number of primaries—go back to the past, as it were.

Primaries are like a lot of things: They work best when people participate. But with dramatically declining rates of voter participation, political officeholders and party leaders can't be pleased with increases in numbers of primaries. The solution is available— to rescind primaries in about a dozen states and switch back to the caucus format until there is a balance between the two systems— 25 each.

Such a shift would permit the political leadership at all levels to regain significance because with their own campaigns they bring to a presidential race contacts, lists, organizers and leaders in other activities such as labor and business that can make the difference in caucuses.

Surely there will not be the numbers of people voting in caucuses even in contrast to primaries that have low turnouts. But all those primaries often do is award delegates and generate a few headlines and TV news reports; they do little if anything to build party structures that in many states have atrophied. And a campaign with compelling issues and a vivid candidate or two would help bring people back into the process—even some campaign veterans who've grown apathetic watching so much of the energy and resources of presidential efforts flow away from the town and ward halls and community centers toward the altar of TV.

In the final report of the Commission on Presidential Nomination and Party Structure of the Democratic National Committee, adopted on Jan. 21 and 22 in 1978, this group had the following to say about a national primary: "The Commission is strongly opposed to proposal for a national primary. Perhaps the most important reason for its opposition is that the commission and the Democratic Party is very concerned that the party maintain its right to regulate its own affairs without congressional interference," interference which would occur if Congress were to institute a national primary.

The commission, which was also referred to as the Winograd Commission, after its chairman Morley Winograd from Michigan, also stated,

A one-day national presidential primary would probably spell the end of the national party system as we know it. . . . A national primary would also favor candidates who already had national reputations and who would buy large chunks of media. It would change the primary system from one con-ducted at the grass roots level in many states to one conducted from television studios of the major cities.

The current primary season gives a lesser known but good candidate a chance to get some small state wins and build momentum. . . . In a national primary the candidate would have to concentrate his or her campaign in the most densely populated states that would yield the most votes.

Although the idea still circulates many years later, there is lit-tle momentum for a national presidential primary. At its core such a concept has little chance of passage, particularly in the U.S. Senate.

It would not be only the senators from the Granite and Hawkeye states who would realize that a national primary would mean much, if not all, of the presidential campaign would bypass the small and medium-sized states. It would not take very long for senators in a place such as Wyoming, with its 494,000 residents, or Vermont, with 609,000 and Alaska, with 627,000 population, to reach the conclusion that their states would not see much of the presidential campaigns while California, with its 34 million resi-dents, and the other megastates would.

Instead of the California Gold Rush of 1849, you'd have a rush for the lode of delegates every quadrennium.

Michael Birkner says that such a change would mean "the fact that the candidates are going to be forced to spend all their money in certain markets and the little states, for example, are just going to get no attention. I don't think that's good for our democracy."

Even with a run-off proviso that would ensure that no one could win the nomination unless they've won a majority of votes, such a format certainly does not allow for a state to conduct a caucus; thus every state would have to be a primary state.

With 40 states conducting presidential primaries in 2000, the observation by Louise Overacker, an assistant professor of history and government at Wellesley College, in her 1926 book *The Presidential Primary*, is still relevant:

> A hoarse, tired candidate whose speeches have lost their spontaneity fails to make a popular appeal and uses up energy which might better be expended in other directions. If the presidential primary should be extended to most of the forty-eight states it would be a physical impossibility for one candidate to cover all of them as intensively as was done by Roosevelt and La Follette in 1912 or by [Leonard] Wood and [Hiram] Johnson in 1920 and the personal appeal would either have to be abandoned or confined to a few strategic points.

A national primary would surely win approval from two groups—owners of television stations in urban markets throughout this nation and political consultants—since such nomination bids would be completely dependent on television exposure.

Writing in *Washington Journalism Review* in December 1987, Larry Sabato, an associate professor of government at the University of Virginia, had this to say about consultants:

> There is no more significant change in the conduct of modern campaigns than the consultant's recent rise to prominence, if not preeminence, during the election season. Political consultants, answerable only to their client-candidate and for the most part independent of the political parties, have inflicted severe damage upon the party system and master-

minded the modern triumph of personality cults over party politics. All the while they have gradually but steadily accumulated almost unchecked and unrivaled power and influence in a system that is partly their handiwork.

While serving as the general chairman of the Democratic National Committee, Connecticut senator Christopher Dodd spoke on March 18, 1995, to a Democratic Party fundraiser in New Hampshire. The day before his speech Dodd told Scot Lehigh of the *Boston Globe* that he was in favor of a New England regional primary for, as Lehigh wrote, such a change "would also give established political figures a leg up on dark horses." Then Dodd added, "I have always believed that this ought not to be a race where the least well-known have an opportunity to do the best. It ought to be a race where people of reputation come, not where you come to make a reputation."

Evidently Dodd, the son of Thomas Dodd, who served in the U.S. Senate from the same state from 1959 to 1971, has an ability to completely rewrite much of the recent history of nomination struggles. The case of Sen. George McGovern toppling frontrunner Sen. Edmund Muskie is an exception. In virtually all cases the frontrunner emerges as the eventual nominee—and that is almost without exception in the GOP.

(Possibly part of the reason for Dodd's rather convoluted logic is that even an astute politician such as Terry Sanford, in his 1981 book *A Danger of Democracy*, referred to New Hampshire McGovern coordinator Joseph Grandmaison, who "was known in his small native state, but he was young and untried, and his victory for McGovern was viewed as a stunning upset." McGovern actually lost the primary by 8,228 votes.)

Martin Gross's opinion on this subject:

When there used to be all this chit-chat about regional

primaries which liberals seemed to like very much, nobody thought about [the fact that] every time you enlarge an electoral process you magnify the money problem. And to run simultaneously in six states is a big job and maybe beyond the capacity of a candidate that is starting out.

One of the glories of the New Hampshire primary used to be that somebody without a whole lot of money but a whole lot of appeal could get in here and by virtue of winning or finishing up there could then get the attention of contributors and the press so as to parlay that into something else. It doesn't work with multi-jurisdictional primaries all on the same day. How do you parlay something small into something big? You don't.

The conceit of New Hampshire is that the process here is not as mass as Mass., if you get my point. And that a little person can still aspire and get in the game. I don't think that's bad. . . . [There would surely be even more effort devoted to trying to attract attention via TV] so that the same damn ad would run everyplace . . . repetitive personal appearances in the big cities wouldn't mean anything.

Sometimes I think there's less and less understanding of what's really going on here in the national media. Television political coverage is just dumb, you know. It's a cartoon. These people have got 90 seconds to do something—they've taken some footage, they chop it up, they get some sort of a theme or somebody blows in their ear and that's their theme—maybe the 90 seconds, if they get 90 seconds. It doesn't communicate how people are reacting to the candidates.

On June 22, 1987, the Democratic Leadership Council (DLC) convened a Super Tuesday Summit in Atlanta, the city where the Democrats would meet in August of the next year to nominate Bay State governor Michael Dukakis.

The handbook for the DLC conclave proclaimed in its initial sentence, "The 1988 presidential election marks the beginning of a new era in American politics."

Later it was noted that "moreover, the nominating races often turn on parochial issues rather than on the broad national concerns that are central to the American people. A process dominated by pressure groups or single-issue activists is certainly no more democratic than one dominated by party regulars."

In the section titled "Beyond Iowa and New Hampshire," the DLC stated,

> Small, unrepresentative and subject to manipulation, the early contests in Iowa and New Hampshire are hardly a conclusive test of any candidate's ability to serve as president. And the manipulation works both ways; recent press accounts show that local candidates or groups are becoming adept at "gaming the system," for example by charging presidential hopefuls—either directly or through campaign contributions to state and local campaigns—to appear before them or to win their support.

Super Tuesday in 1988 managed to encompass 20 states, 14 of which were in or bordering the South. Just over a third of the Democrats' (37%) delegates were awarded that single day, the closest this nation has ever come to a de facto national primary.

A couple of observers later wrote of this mega-event, "Super Tuesday in 1988 was so big a political event on paper that it obscured its own meaning."

The DLC noted that candidates are quickly "written off by the news media as hopeless also rans—although just a tiny fraction of the voters have been heard from—with many more states yet to be counted."

Therefore the first caucus and primary lead to the following:

Premature obituaries, litmus tests, thinly disguised political shakedowns and obsessive media attention on small, preliminary events—these circumstances hardly create an atmosphere for a high quality debate on national needs and priorities. The American people deserve better. At the very least, they deserve a substantive debate among the candidates on the most pressing challenges facing our country.

In an interview with the *Washington Post National Weekly* published just a few weeks after the vote on March 8, 1988, Virginia senator Charles Robb (who in 2000 was defeated in a try for a third term) proclaimed,

> I was one of the architects . . . to give voters in the participating states a greater voice in the selecting of nominees of both parties and, of even greater importance, to force the candidates to face a broader and more typical electorate. Super Tuesday was designed to be the first authentic test of the candidates' ability to mount a national campaign. . . . In my judgment, the success of Super Tuesday bodes well for the party's chances in November.

As George Will pointed out a week after the November election: "Democrats devised Super Tuesday to force their candidates to court the South early in the nomination process. They held their convention in the South. They plucked their vice-presidential nominee from the South. They lost the South and the border, 155–0."

Perhaps the saddest testimonial to the "wonders" of Super Tuesday in 1988 was a television report of how Missouri congressman Dick Gephardt spent almost an entire day just before the vote. While he sat in a hotel he spent hour after hour conducting interviews with TV stations spread across the region. It was a far cry from being on the hustings in Iowa or New Hampshire.

In another context, columnist Michael Tomasky of *New York* magazine on July 8, 2002, wrote about the failure of thinking on too grand a scale:

> If anything, largeness usually gets in the way of great-ness. History suggests to us that size can work up to a certain point, after which the bigger something is, the less likely it is to serve an ennobling and appropriately demotic purpose. There was, ironically, no better proof of the theorem than the Twin Towers themselves. We mourn their demise, of course, but as we consider the future we'd do well to keep in mind not only the awful way they went down but the unsavory political shakedowns that were behind the way they went up. Nobody in New York except three men, two of whom happened to be named Rockefeller (the third was Port Authority chief Austin Tobin), wanted buildings that big.

After yet another attempt in early March to hold numerous primaries on a single day, *Boston Globe* columnist Thomas Oliphant wrote on April 15, 1992: "The answer to deteriorating democracy is better democracy. For starters, the frontloading of primaries should stop; a better spread of voting dates would end the tarmac campaigns epitomized by the colossal failure of Super Tuesday."

Asked if he thought the nomination process would be improved if there was a balance once again between primaries and caucuses, Bill Gardner answered,

> I think so. I know that goes against the motherhood and apple pie slogans that we want more people to be part of this process . . . the more people that you have involved in this process—the primary process—the better. . . . In order to have more people involved you have to come up with a system that

doesn't end up limiting the choices that those people are going to have. What good is it if you have many, many people involved but the choices for most of those people are decreasing because fewer people [candidates] can participate?

Asked for his opinion of what is taking place as concerns the evolving nomination system, Michael Birkner stated,

I do believe that the presidential nomination system needs some sanity. I'm very strongly of the opinion that the way that the Democrats and the Republicans are going is essentially on a highway to hell for American politics. The whole idea of frontloading major states within a matter of a week or two after Iowa caucuses and New Hampshire has its primary makes no sense if you're going to think of democracy in connection with the word deliberation. . . .

[In analyzing what happened in the '50s and '60s]: The virtue of the system was that New Hampshire could be an indicator, it could give a boost to a candidate, it could tell a candidate you've got to change gears, but it didn't *kill* the candidate who lost and it didn't assure the nomination to a candidate who won. That seems pretty reasonable to me. The system now is geared for chaos. Chaos oddly enough out, I think, of an early nomination because when I say chaos I mean there's no deliberative system whereby the voter can get used to the candidate and make a decision.

We're going to get a situation—if we go in the direction we're going right now—we're going to get a situation where a candidate is going to come forward and be nominated in effect by March, and the electorate and the party is going to realize by May—oops—we've got the wrong guy. And that could be a disaster for this country.

Given the sizable amounts of money now required to become a legitimate presidential contender, the role of fundraisers is crucial, and some contend we've changed a system controlled by political bosses and captains of industry to one now dominated by fundraisers.

Walter Peterson, who served as governor from 1969 to 1973, was interviewed in the documentary "The Premier Primary." Peterson backed maverick John McCain in the last primary and he said of the opposition to the first primary,

> Well, the backroom is a money backroom and those are the people who want to kill the New Hampshire primary because they are very resentful of the fact that there's this small state, it doesn't do what you're supposed to do, it's supposed to do what we want you to do. We're supposed to pull the strings and you're supposed to jump. . . . It's the last remaining place where retail politics can be practiced and the nation has a chance to see if some alternative to the preferred candidate by the party organization will raise his or her head.

In a discussion paper for the National Association of Secretaries of State in May 1996, one of this nation's leading experts on the nomination process, Mark A. Siegel, wrote,

> During the fifties and in 1960, the presidential nominating process took on a rather familiar and rational shape, almost identical for both the Democratic and Republican parties. Four or five definitive primaries emerged, first in New Hampshire, to winnow down the field of candidates to a serious two or three. Survivors would then be tested against each other in an orderly series of state primaries—Illinois, Wisconsin, West Virginia, Pennsylvania and ultimately California on the first Tuesday in June.

[Siegel bemoaned the decline of the caucus]: This movement to primaries accelerates over the years—more than thirty
by 1980 and over forty in 1992. Under the current system in
use, party caucuses have become increasingly irrelevant, with
no large state employing this method of delegate selection.
Only the first-in-the-nation Iowa caucuses (we are discounting
the Louisiana system since almost all of the Republican presidential field boycotted it) continues to play a significant role in
the presidential nomination process.

In late January 2002, the Democratic National Committee
decided to move the permitted period for primaries and caucuses
other than Iowa and the Granite State from the first Tuesday in
March to the first Tuesday in February. Siegel's observation in 1996
that "the period between the end of March, when the nominee is
functionally selected, and the opening of the national convention
in the summer, become potential 'dead weight'—a twilight zone of
disinterest that could chill political participation in the fall" is
quite prescient.

Washington Post columnist David Broder wrote of the DNC's
latest rules revision,

With virtually no public debate, the nominating calendar
was changed to guarantee that even more states will hold delegate primaries even earlier in the winter of '04 than in 2000.
Every party official and campaign strategist I talked to agrees
that the race to choose the next Democratic nominee will begin
in earnest less than a year from now, as soon as the midterm
election is out of the way.

In *The Vanishing Voter*, Thomas E. Patterson, the Bradlee professor of Government and the Press at Harvard's John F. Kennedy
School of Government, seems as unhappy about this change as
columnist Broder. He wrote,

In 2001, DNC national chairman Terry McAuliffe engineered a new calendar for the 2004 election that will exacerbate the voters' problems. With virtually no public debate, he persuaded the DNC to approve a calendar that will move Iowa and New Hampshire a week closer to the beginning of the year and allow any other state to hold its primary as early as February 3. The pause after New Hampshire will be only one week, rather than the five weeks in 2000, and if a large number of states move into the early February date, Super Tuesday will occur a month earlier than in 2000. McAuliffe's goal is a quick conclusion to the nominating race so that Democrats can prepare for what he says "will be a tough fight against an incumbent with unlimited finances."

The DNC failed to consider a change in its rules that would certainly have brought some regional balance to the nomination process. At the same time they could have taken a step to mitigate the negative effects of frontloading. All that would have been necessary was to permit the Democrats to hold a primary in South Carolina a week after New Hampshire's (the GOP in South Carolina has followed soon after the Granite State since 1980), and permit a western state to hold a primary or caucus a week after South Carolina.

Such a revision would have eliminated the complaint that having the two traditional states at the outset of the presidential parade had a deal of unfairness for candidates from the South and the West.

Bill Gardner said that he met Terry McAuliffe shortly after he was elected chairman of the DNC and

I got the feeling that he wanted to change very little from what was in the past—except for those states that had tried to lobby him for their own state concerns. I didn't get the feeling that he was interested in taking the party on another McGovern–Fraser Commission [the first nomination reform group formed just after the 1968 election] or Winograd Commission or another attempt to revamp the process.

With the march toward a frontloaded system continuing without much resistance from national party leaders, one could ask if there is an agenda here. The parties have done a masterful job in the past few decades of turning the national conventions, which used to offer some suspense and—dare it be said—excitement—into four nights of packaged and programmed entertainment that is about as compelling to watch as much of the network fare on TV.

This country hasn't seen a multiballot convention since the Democrats went to three ballots in 1952 and the GOP also went three rounds in 1948. This is not a call for a return to the good old days of the 103 ballots it took the Democrats to nominate John Davis in 1924; having the nomination fight wrapped up in the first few weeks of caucuses and primaries helps to unify the parties—but at what cost to a vital and vibrant democracy? And does this cut-and-dried system that further tilts the nomination process toward the frontrunner only cement the control the consultants, fundraisers and party leaders have—once again to the detriment of the electorate?

Will the system be that much better if the process is over in the blink of an eye as far as the actual voting on the candidates is concerned—and the real decision making lies elsewhere?

In his 1996 paper, Mark Siegel wrote,

The Democrats' failure to successfully address the frontloading problem in the 1970s and 1980s may be viewed in retrospect as one of the greatest missed opportunities in American politics to prevent a predicted systemic crisis in the future.

The fundamental consequence of the frontloading of both parties' delegate selection systems is the finality of the judgment that is achieved in very few weeks. The old system allowed for introspection and reevaluation. The new calendar all but prohibits revisiting decisions within the party. A flawed candidate who may be about to come unglued may quickly go over the delegate selection majority number even as it is becoming obvious to analysts that he is unelectable.

It would not take congressional nor even national party action to mitigate some of the negative impacts that frontloading has had on our political process.

With the size of this nation and the inability of candidates to campaign everywhere, more and more states will finally realize that very few can conduct a New Hampshire–style primary.

Party leaders can continue to study the abysmal turnout figures in both presidential and state primary elections and conclude that if just about a dozen small and medium-sized states shift from presidential primaries to caucuses they will have taken a crucial step toward restoring some balance in the process.

There would be no better way to stanch the flow of money toward television advertising than for more states to return to the caucus format.

In addition, there would be no better way to invigorate the parties on the grassroots level than to make such a change: Drawing voters to caucus meetings is surely a better way to engage new activists in the process than simply giving them the chance to enter a voting booth and mark up a ballot.

Caucuses involve a lengthy process that moves from the local to county to congressional districts and then a state convention over several months; this spread-out system would reduce the media-driven rush to judgment that Siegel bemoaned.

In addition, both parties could include a bonus provision (say

10% or 15%) for any state that shifts to a caucus; this enticement could act as a catalyst in a movement toward a system with an equal number of primaries and caucuses.

In the 2000 election, only two major states—Texas and Michigan—used the caucus format and it was only the Democrats in those two states who did so. To make matters even more confusing, Texas Democrats held a primary and a caucus on the same day. (They allotted 127 delegates in the primary and 67 in the caucus.) Given the expense and logistical nightmare it can become in a megastate, a caucus is far more suitable for the smaller states.

Furthermore, a caucus (except, unfortunately, in Iowa) has minimal use for television advertising (no small feat) and thus would put a premium on grassroots organizing, something as nearly extinct in many states as carbon paper.

As the New World Primary Order continues, it is still possible that party leaders in small states will conclude that if they switch back to a caucus they may find a more suitable place in the nomination scheme than they have now.

It is hoped that the national political leadership in both parties will someday realize that taking a wrecking ball to Iowa's and New Hampshire's contests would prove to be a mistake.

Indeed, with Super Tuesday events (and don't forget Junior Tuesday and Titanic Tuesday) held since 1980, enough evidence is in to conclude that holding an election on a single day with almost a third of the nation involved is democracy in name only. In practice it ends up being a television extravaganza that leaves very few content with the outcome or even the manner in which the election was conducted.

On August 31, 2000, the Committee for the Study of the American Electorate (CSAE) issued a report on the problem with frontloading and the increasing disengagement that year that created the second lowest primary turnout, among other matters.

Written by the director of CSAE, Curtis Gans, the report stated in part,

> Something needs to be done about the virtual abdication of the coverage of politics by the major networks and their affiliates. In the pre–Super Tuesday primary period, there were 20 prime-time debates. Not one was covered by network television. The average audience for those prime-time debates on PBS and cable was 1.5 million. The average audience for a prime-time entertainment show on one network is 9 million and 42 million for all four. Debates for lower offices are almost always ignored by network affiliates but provide the best means of presenting the candidates and cutting through the distortions of political advertising. . . . We have had during the last decade an almost 70 percent reduction in the amount of time given to politics on the nightly news during campaigns. Presidents find they must give afternoon press conferences to get three minutes on the nightly news, when once these conferences and responses were part of the broadcasters' responsibility. . . .
>
> The present system has many flaws, including limiting candidacy to the famous, the rich and those with access to wealth; lengthening the ersatz campaign so that candidates must start running to raise money at least a year before any actual votes are cast and making journalists and media events more determinative than voters; reducing the political scrutiny of candidates for the most powerful position in the world; emphasizing the worst aspects of campaigning—the attack ad and tarmac campaigns which follow the Iowa and New Hampshire events; creating a long demobilizing political dead space after the climactic primaries; and denying flexibility to the process to make mid-stream corrections.

If there is anyone in this country who believes there is any hope that the three major networks will ever return to a policy of substantial coverage of American politics, they need to be reminded of just one fact: In October 2002, when George W. Bush appeared on the David Letterman show, he received as much airtime as he and Gore had garnered on all three networks combined in that month.

Is there any reason to believe that the three major networks will provide much in the way of coverage in 2004 if the minutes of campaign coverage decreased from 1,474 minutes in 1992 to just 805 in 2000, according to a tracking by the Center for Media and Public Affairs and the Brookings Institution?

The same groups produce a tracking of how horse race coverage dominates the news coverage by the three major networks: In the general election in 2000, 71% of the stories were about the horse race; in 1996, it was 48%.

One of the failures of the modern era of presidential campaigning is the loss of hope that the expansion of TV into virtually every home in this country would lead to an electronic town hall of sorts where millions upon millions of Americans could learn about the candidates, the issues and the major (and even minor) political parties and then render an informed judgment on Election Day.

TV was supposed to reduce the need for candidates to engage in the ritual of glad-handing and the like because they could not reach a mass media audience.

Yet what James W. Davis wrote in the book *Springboard to the White House* in 1967 regarding the 1912 effort for the GOP nomination by former president Theodore Roosevelt against his successor, President William Howard Taft, is still valid: "Roosevelt set out on one of the most strenuous pre-convention campaigns in history. From March to June he personally invaded every primary state but Wisconsin, speaking as often as ten times a day. By the end of his campaign, with his oxlike strength, T.R. was near exhaustion."

Therefore, instead of men such as T.R., Estes Kefauver and Jimmy Carter roaming the countryside for months on end foraging for votes and delegates, TV would mean a new way to campaign, a far more effective way to reach the millions of voters of this nation.

It hasn't quite worked out that way. When Neal Peirce was asked what has happened with this new medium of mass communications he had this succinct response: "It got used the way it's used and cheapened as a medium."

After all, the three major networks have reduced their gavel-to-gavel coverage to just a couple of hours for four evenings each quadrennium—not each year, mind you.

The three major networks can't seem to trouble themselves with any coverage of debates in the important caucus and primary tests other than an occasional sound bite from what someone said.

And time and time again the networks provide more airtime for their correspondents than they do for the candidates they are attempting to cover.

No doubt there will continue to be studies, reports, seminars, books, hearings, lectures and pamphlets on what ails our process of selecting a president of the United States.

However, the remedy is not a New Hampshirization of the process—with more primaries added to the 40 in 2000—for that would only mean the failure of success from a state that has held a presidential primary since 1916.

If the nomination tussle isn't over quickly in 2004, obviously the states holding caucuses will find themselves subject to candidate and media attention—perhaps to a far greater degree than if they tried to conduct a primary.

An advantage of a shift toward a more balanced system of caucuses and primaries is that in the event of buyer's remorse there will still be an opportunity to make a correction. If someone gallivants through the first month of the process only to discover that he has too much luggage to have a chance of winning on the first Tuesday in November, the more balanced system has built into it a check whereby approximately two dozen states slowly winding their way through the complex caucus format can conduct a process of review that simply isn't always possible in states that have held primaries—particularly the megastates.

A system that would permit a leisurely stroll out of the snows of the Granite State and then on to a week or two of stumping in states such as Wisconsin, Pennsylvania, West Virginia, Oregon and a few other primaries until the "Super Bowl of primaries" in California in early June has gone the way of the 3¢ postage stamp.

In the Sept. 15, 1995, issue of the *Boston Globe*, David Shribman (who became the executive editor of the *Pittsburgh Post-Gazette* in February 2003) wrote,

> Political campaigns are much like wars: Truth is the first casualty. But parts of the New Hampshire myth are true. The activists care desperately. The candidates work the state furiously. The state's boosters defend their primary ferociously. But the sad fact is that New Hampshire has become more like the rest of the country. The pity of it all is that the process didn't work the other way around.

But with 39 other states trying to duplicate the New Hampshire primary experience, too many states have managed to follow the wrong model. As much as it pains me to write this, the future of the nominating process may well be in the Midwest and not here in northern New England. Surely something needs to be done to add to the vigor of our democracy, and it seems clearer with each passing presidential election that our democracy is being damaged by a surplus of presidential primaries.

If this nation were to return to a balanced system with about 25 primaries and the same number of caucuses, because these caucuses would be *sans* TV ad blitzes if sanity manages to prevail, we would be well on the way to curing a process that has become far too expensive, too exhausting, too boring, too trite and with far too few opportunities for the people to learn more about those seeking the highest office in the land and for those candidates to learn about those they hope to govern.

No doubt if more states began to shift back to caucuses this state would not be among them. But if this change does take place it will go a long way toward restoring what is needed more and more: Candidates would be able to return to what was once a more measured test through every region of this land.

That would be a worthwhile change to strive for.

At some point the two major parties may decide that New Hampshire will have to share the first primary spot with a Southern state, a Midwestern one and a Western state.

If this change were made, would the kaffeeklatsch experience that takes place here and in Iowa begin to show up on the candidate schedules in, say, Georgia, Michigan and Washington?

Sharing the first primary date with three other states would surely heighten many of the negative aspects of frontloading. Candidates would be even more desperate than they are now to make some sort of breakthrough in order to generate the media momentum and inflow of money to compete after the first primary date.

On Nov. 20, 1999, the Democratic National Committee held the first of four hearings on possible changes to the presidential nomination calendar for the 2004 election.

Sen. Carl Levin, a Democrat from Michigan and a persistent opponent of Iowa's and New Hampshire's roles, called such a situation "fundamentally wrong." He inquired, "Why should two states have this kind of impact? Any two states?"

To the surprise of no one in New Hampshire, Gov. Jeanne

Shaheen told the conclave of her support for the status quo. New Hampshire secretary of state Bill Gardner testified to the historic role the primary has played since 1920.

Also speaking was Senator Levin's older brother (by three years), Sander, who has been a congressman from Michigan since 1983. (Carl Levin first won a Senate seat in 1978.)

Representative Levin discounted the contention by the two early-bird states that their residents in their residences were able to ask "person, character type of questions." He was then quoted by Associated Press as saying, "I think people in living rooms ask frank questions no matter where they live . . ."

One could say that a living room is a living room no matter whether it is located in Andover, New Hampshire (pop. 1,883), or Ann Arbor, Michigan (111,300) or Atlanta, Georgia (394,017). But is it really?

Once the first primary is held, the grassroots element disappears, to be replaced by the tarmac-to-tarmac mad dash around the country and the information flow is transformed into an all-media all-the-time extravaganza.

Do each party's two major contenders often left standing after the first direct vote spend much of the time in living rooms in the weeks following the New Hampshire determination? Certainly not.

A change to four primaries on the first day would only result in even more power for the media to shape the destiny of the nomination race.

The voters always seem to find a challenger to the media-anointed frontrunner; otherwise, the press would have to pack up their bags and leave the campaign trail to return to the thrilling task of covering Congress and the federal bureaucracy.

Another step to enhance the role of the media is not something to be encouraged, as Thomas Patterson wrote in his 1993 book *Out of Order*: "Some of the developments in election journalism over the past two decades have represented an improvement. However, the trend that elevated the journalist's voice to a position above that of the candidate is not among them."

The conclusion that any change that enlarges the pool of voters manages at the same time to drown out the voice of the voting populace only adds to the power of the press and weakens our democracy.

In the end what matters is who is given the opportunity to step up on the stage and state his or her case to the nation. Because of fame or fortune, a Rockefeller, Kennedy, Glenn, Forbes or Reagan has ample opportunity to make his pitch to the voters.

If permitted to do so, the press will take so much space on that platform that in the end the lesser known and long shots will simply be shunted aside.

Or, as scholar Patterson also wrote in his 1993 book: "It presumes that the press, rather than the candidate, should be charged with defining the public's choices. The media are in no position to act as the voters' representatives. They can serve as the voters' watchdog, but not as their trustee."

If the DNC and RNC did decide to permit three other states in different regions to vote on the same day as the Granite State, and one of those states just happened to be Michigan, would the aspirants find their way to the living rooms that Representative Levin spoke about in November 1999?

Indeed, early in the campaign, without Secret Service protection or a media posse filling one or two buses, no doubt candidates could show up in Representative Levin's hometown of Royal Oak, population 66,900, to the north and a bit west of Detroit, and complete a schedule very similar to what is done here.

But Michigan isn't New Hampshire; it does, after all, have 10 million residents. Just how long would a campaign manager in the national headquarters keep his or her job in the fall and early winter as the campaign built up a head of steam, if the manager insisted that the campaign maintain a schedule for the first primary that was the same format as for any other state?

It would have to be chock-a-block full of the meet-and-greet conducted here since 1952, when Estes Kefauver helped put the decision here on the map: the coffees; the Rotary Club speeches; the visits to address senior citizens, high school and college students; the walking tours of downtown areas; the drop-bys at the local newspaper and radio station; and maybe a press conference or some one-on-one with reporters in tow.

That same type of schedule isn't even logistically possible in a state as large as Michigan, because the media always completely surround those lucky enough to capture the imagination of the voters, and they would be totally oblivious to the reality of a campaign in modern America.

Just how long would a campaign manager stay on the job if the schedule in Michigan was essentially the same as that in the kick-off state?

Sometimes a frontrunner or strong contender will have 40 or 50 requests daily for interviews from local, regional, statewide, national and international media. Can a candidate be oblivious to such requests and instead stick to a schedule that has three or four coffees in a day?

There is an enormous difference between trying to win delegates from a ministate primary and a megastate one. As long as this country maintains an understanding of the vast difference between the smallest and the largest, we will be able to provide a system that still permits a way for the lesser known to become one of the better known. It is unfortunate that Senator Levin and Congressman Levin can't seem to grasp this concept.

Some reporter covering a candidate in this campaign should do the following: When traveling in New Hampshire the reporter should carry a stopwatch and at every meeting the candidate holds that the reporter is permitted access to, the stopwatch should be used to total the time spent in Q and A with the public.

When the reporter then follows a candidate to a megastate he or she should do the same thing. In all meetings the would-be president holds with the public, the reporter should just pull out the stopwatch and once again add up the amount of time in Q and A with John Q. Public.

In all the megastates and many of the middle-sized states the media become a filter or barrier between the candidate and the populace. There were those who hoped that while spending about $3 million in the 1996 primary Steve Forbes would prove that New Hampshire had become much like the rest of the nation. But, alas, even after all that money and speculation by some pundits that this state had become media fixated like so much of the rest of this nation, Forbes proved to be no heir of the Reagan legacy and finished a dismal fourth place.

Although the media (in particular, TV 9) have become an important component of the vote, this locale is still a throwback to another time when there was some sort of a rough equivalence between the political leadership, the press and the public. And our democracy is the better for it.

V

OF PRIMARY SIGNIFICANCE

The principal failures in the war in Vietnam were not military failures. They were failures by civilian leaders of this country to determine policy, to give direction and set limits, to take the diplomatic action necessary to bring the war to an end, and to act responsibly without regard for what such an ending might be called—defeat, surrender, victory, or stalemate.

—Eugene McCarthy, *The Hard Years*

A FEW DAYS PRIOR to the 1988 primary, while I was speaking to a group at the New Hampshire Historical Society in Concord, a woman asked what I thought had been the most significant New Hampshire presidential primary.

Without hesitation I answered: 1968—the Democratic contest. I did not move to this state until 1969 and was a college student in southern California when Sen. Eugene McCarthy almost defeated President Lyndon Johnson; therefore, I had no first-person investment in what had taken place here on March 12, 1968.

This wasn't a question I dealt with in my book *First in the Nation*. There seemed to be so much to cover in the nine primaries the book deals with from 1952 to 1984 that I don't recall ever asking anyone in the more than 100 interviews conducted (all but one of which are at the New Hampshire Historical Society) the question that was asked of me in 1988.

So the answer given that afternoon in the capital city was very much off-the-cuff, something provided more on instinct than either research or deliberation before answering.

In the preparation of this book I have been asking that question. However, I always try to make sure the question is phrased the same way each time: Which New Hampshire primary do you believe has been the most significant to the nation?

The individuals questioned are not asked what has been the most significant to them personally, or to the political party they may belong to, or even to this state. It is an attempt to discern which primary, more than any other, has helped shape the destiny of the United States of America.

Asked which particular primary has been the most significant to the nation, Michael Birkner responded,

> I think 1952 would have to be the most significant because if New Hampshire had voted for Taft against Eisenhower in '52 there would have been no Eisenhower presidential campaign. I think there was a direct cause and effect. Eisenhower would have insisted that he was not interested in running for the nomination and would have withdrawn his name from further primaries.
>
> That changes an era because if Eisenhower was not in the mix in 1952 you're either going to have another Democratic administration under Stevenson, which could have been uglier than the second Truman administration, or you would have had a very weak Republican president because there wasn't anybody in Eisenhower's league on the Republican side. So that changes the nation. I think it changes history.

There seems to be a bit too much hypothetical content in Dr. Birkner's answer. The same phenomenon takes place when a couple of people have responded to the question asked of Birkner: the election of '76.

That response goes something like this: If only one fewer liberal had run here, Arizona representative Morris Udall would have emerged the victor rather than the moderate Jimmy Carter. Therefore, the theory goes, Udall as the Democratic nominee would have been able to defeat President Gerald Ford (something I have my doubts about) and he surely would have been a better president than Jimmy Carter (something I have no doubt about).

A few people have mentioned the GOP race in 1980 but not with much enthusiasm. President Reagan surely changed the course of the federal government in a more conservative direction, but given the increase in the federal debt he left and the taint of the Iran-Contra scandal, it is difficult to place him in the pantheon of great or even near-great presidents.

During this informal survey no other primary has come up. It is a question that has been posed to only about two dozen people, and maybe at some time some educational or media institution in the Granite State will compile a list of 100 or 125 New Hampshire citizens to grapple with this question.

Some will ask how I, who participated in or observed every primary since 1972, settled on 1968 and the Democratic one at that. As pointed out in the first chapter, Senator McCarthy, who'd won his first of two terms in 1958 from his native Minnesota, lost this primary by 4,251 votes to the write-in for President Johnson. The senator did win 20 of the 24 delegates, but that was because there were far more Johnson delegate hopefuls on the ballots than there were for McCarthy, who had been on the short list of vice presidential possibilities considered by Lyndon Johnson in 1964.

Senator McCarthy won 601 delegates at the Chicago convention in August, a convention so out of control it can be considered one of the defining events of the campaign and therefore a major reason former vice president Richard Nixon finally achieved the presidency—this time over Vice President Hubert Humphrey, who had won the Democratic nomination with 1,759 convention votes.

One of the veterans of the McCarthy bid here said that for many individuals what transpired in March 1968 was the defining experience of their lives. And it was acknowledged that few, if any, realized it at the time. So much happened afterward that helped shape the destiny of this nation that it is doubtful that the 23,269 votes McCarthy tallied here could have had the impact in any other state in a year that saw so much death and tragedy for this country—both at home and in Vietnam.

The process has become such a maze of fundraising, months (if not years) on the campaign trail, campaign staffs the size of corporations, plus countless consultants to shape not just the message of the campaign, but the candidate's attire and so often, it seems, his thoughts, that the McCarthy campaign retains an aura that, while not bliss, comes close to that.

That effort in 1968 did not achieve victory in New Hampshire, Chicago or on November 5. Yet it did change the direction of this nation for the better and it did help bring about the beginning of the end for this nation's military involvement in Vietnam. For me it really isn't a close call as to which New Hampshire presidential primary more than any other has been the most significant to this nation.

Anyone who studies that primary campaign can only be struck by how simple and direct it was. How small the staff was and how unencumbered the candidate was by managers, consultants, operatives, spokesmen and the like. Gene McCarthy was a man with a message, who delivered it in an understated manner (which drove the press that took the time to cover him here mad). Rather than drive a stake through the heart of the administration of Lyndon Johnson, he preferred the more indirect route of talking sense to the voters of this state and left it up to them as to what was the best way to tell President Johnson (just as the same state had told President Truman in 1952) it was time for him to go.

I was asked once by Merv Weston of Manchester, the public relations executive not only for McCarthy here but also George McGovern in 1972 and Mo Udall in 1976, just what type of president McCarthy would have been.

I make no claim to being a presidential scholar and was not here to watch him campaign, but I had seen enough of McCarthy after 1968 that I told Weston I did not believe he'd have been like several of the presidents we'd had. I thought he'd have performed more like the prime minister of Great Britain. I doubt that a President McCarthy would have tried to put his stamp on this country as Franklin Roosevelt, John Kennedy, Lyndon Johnson or even Ronald Reagan tried to do.

His approach would have been far more circumspect and he never would have been accused of trying to conduct an imperial presidency.

(I added that if McCarthy had indeed become president there's absolutely no doubt he would have pushed for the enactment of some form of national health insurance.)

As every presidential election begins, reporters and pundits often search for a previous campaign to serve as a model for the one about to unfold. Sometimes the year selected does actually fit.

Right now there is a debate as to whether the 2004 election should be modeled after the 1992 one as the Democrats would no doubt prefer; 1972 is the race the Republicans would like to see replicated.

It would be difficult to find a year such as 1968 that was so closely matched with 1952—especially as regards the outcome in the initial primary.

In both years a Democratic president was driven from a reelection effort: In 1952 Harry Truman dropped out 18 days after being upset by Tennessee senator Estes Kefauver by just 3,873 votes. In 1968 Lyndon Johnson withdrew 19 days after his near-defeat by Eugene McCarthy.

Both presidential administrations were hobbled by prolonged military campaigns in Asia. The difference was that Johnson's withdrawal had a great deal to do with Vietnam, whereas Truman's decision not to seek a second full term was made with the Korean War not quite reaching the national crisis that Vietnam would for LBJ 16 years later.

Yet the earlier war did not feature the bitter intra- and inter-party contention that Vietnam managed to generate.

For example, Ohio senator Robert Taft, a Republican with long-held isolationist sentiments, said at one press conference what he would have done if he had been president when South Korea was attacked in June 1950: "I would have stayed out." And as the casualties mounted during the invasion of North Korea, his answer to the query about what to do then was a simple one: "I think I would get out and fall back to a defensible position in Japan and Formosa."

Joseph Bruce Gorman wrote in his 1971 biography of Kefauver,

> But Kefauver himself became increasingly unhappy with what appeared to be both a military and political quagmire and was on occasion mildly critical of the Administration. . . . It was this feeling that no end was in sight that bothered Kefauver most, and, although he never made the Korean War an issue in his campaigns within the party against Truman or Truman-backed favorite sons, he did temporarily urge a threat of greater military force in the hope of influencing the communists to accept an end to the fighting.

Therefore, the Korean War never became quite as involved in an American presidential campaign as the Vietnam War did in 1968 as well as in 1972.

A similarity between these two wars was the debate that continued for many years afterward as to whether this nation had pulled its punches. Was our military strength so circumscribed that we failed to fully utilize our naval, air and nuclear capabilities to shorten each war and save a substantial number of American lives?

In both elections considered here, there was an opportunity for the electorate to embrace the more hawkish position. The name of Gen. Douglas MacArthur had been entered in the 1952 GOP presidential preference poll, but he had it withdrawn and urged his supporters to vote for Senator Taft rather than his former assistant, Dwight Eisenhower.

MacArthur was the beneficiary of a write-in effort. The result: He garnered a mere 3,227 votes, just 3.5%.

Alabama governor George Wallace could easily have entered the Democratic primary here in 1968. Just 50 names in each of the two congressional districts was required then. Although there are still those who wish to portray this state as some sort of Mississippi of the North, Wallace surely wasn't one of them, for he skipped the vote here. He fared worse than MacArthur: He tallied just 504 write-in votes, 0.4%.

Allowing the voters to use the candidates to register their opinion of a war overseas is a procedure that can be conducted in a megastate as well as it can in a ministate such as New Hampshire.

But in the end the larger contest takes place in a venue that permits little if any face-to-face campaigning with ordinary voters. This means a playing field that is slanted toward those in power—and what is the point in asking who should lead this land of ours if the outcome is essentially already determined?

Time and time again this small state has one of the highest turnout rates for federal and state elections in the nation. Yet it is still far from a complete democracy, for in every election thousands of citizens can't be bothered with voting.

It can also create some bemusement when the TV networks start to display the vote totals for candidates on primary night;

then it becomes obvious, even when all the votes are tabulated and the winners (and near-winners) are proclaimed, that it is still just a tiny fraction of votes compared to so many other states in the Union.

Just one candidate—John McCain in 2000—has ever succeeded in breaking the 100,000 vote barrier: with 115,606. Critics of the role this state plays cite the miniscule number of voters to question why such a tiny state has such an inordinate amount of clout in our nomination system.

However, because there are so few voters, the human elements of reaching out to the voters—the walking tours of the main streets, greeting workers at factories, the speeches to Rotary Clubs and high schools, as opposed to so many TV interviews and ads in most other states—mean that this state is still a very different political environment.

The voters of the Granite State don't decide who the next president will be. They do decide who the rest of the nation will decide on as to who the nominees of our two major parties will be.

In 1968 Eugene McCarthy managed to tally just 23,269 votes, 4,251 fewer votes than the write-in for President Lyndon Johnson. Really not much of a vote total in the grand scheme of things.

As they say, an awful lot was going on at that time, with the worst news for the American public coming from the first televised war commencing with the Tet offensive in late January and then a succession of reports out of Saigon and Washington that made it clear the price for winning in Vietnam was becoming steeper with every passing day.

There does happen to be here a very fine line (as there is so often in war) between victory and defeat, a line so thin sometimes that candidates such as McCarthy (and George McGovern in 1972) lose by so few votes that the press reaches a conclusion that the second-place finisher is in fact a moral victor.

However, that happens only when the frontrunner fails to

match expectations and his most serious challenger manages to exceed his.

With such a miniscule electorate there have been a number of close races. This in the end leads to a great deal of "what if" speculation concerning the outcome of several contests—particularly the GOP primary in 1976.

As noted columnist George Will wrote in *Newsweek* in March 1976,

> If 794 New Hampshire Republicans had voted the other way, Ford would have limped into Florida a loser. That probably would have meant three percent more of the vote for Ronald Reagan, and a second Ford loss. But that destiny was derailed by those 794 voters, and Ford's presidency has entered a prosperous new phase.

One could ask what might have happened eight years prior to that close contest if just 2,000 more New Hampshire voters had voted for Lyndon Johnson instead of Senator McCarthy.

Instead, the outcome would have been 53% for Johnson, 38% for McCarthy. Thus McCarthy would have failed to reach the 40% benchmark set for him late in the campaign by the leader of the Johnson write-in here, Bernard Boutin: "It would be a disgrace if McCarthy gets less than 40% of the vote."

How much of our political history could have been changed if McCarthy had not achieved the status of moral victory will never be known. But one can be reasonably sure that for each percentage point that McCarthy fell below 40% the spin machine of an entire administration would have been ready to let the country know just what a remarkable achievement it was for the Johnson effort to win by such a comfortable margin.

It is clear that if there had been no first primary here on March 12 and also no primaries in a dozen other states until the final one on June 11 in Illinois, this country would have been on a far different and much more dangerous path than 1968 turned out to be. Which is saying something, for that year, with the assassinations of the Rev. Martin Luther King Jr. on April 4 and Robert Kennedy on June 5, this land of ours was in a world of turmoil and violence.

That turned out to be the year the primaries proved to be of more value to this nation than before or afterward. A closed political system was challenged and opened up to participation of millions galvanized by their opposition to the war. They challenged the established order but used peaceful means and the democratic process to do so. And that campaign served as invaluable training for a new generation of political leaders to eventually emerge.

What if there had been no presidential primaries in 1968—no place for all that anger and frustration and dismay so many felt about the Vietnam War, a conflict many in this country would never have called a just war. It is likely that fall election would have more closely resembled the violence-prone contests that marred so many elections in the last century in South America.

The final authority on whether to send even more troops to Vietnam rested in the hands of one person—Lyndon Baines Johnson. But the votes in the first primary on March 12, 1968, managed to check his power.

In his memoir of his presidency *The Vantage Point*, published in 1971, President Johnson wrote of the possible huge increase of troops, "The fact was I had firmly decided against sending approaching 206,000 additional men to Vietnam and already had so informed my senior advisors."

The troop increase was much smaller, but New Hampshire with only a tiny fraction of the votes cast that year in this nation surely helped place our nation on a different path. It was, after all, the decision that started the process to end our involvement in Vietnam and it did breathe new life into our democratic system.

Who knows whether the 2004 New Hampshire presidential primary will indeed turn out to be the final first-in-the-nation vote? One can be certain that if it does turn out to be the last one, the replacement will not provide the level playing field that has served this nation so well for so long.

There is little doubt that whatever the alternative ends up being it will diminish—not, as the Granite State has managed to accomplish for so long for this republic of ours—enhance our presidential election system.

New Hampshire Presidential Primary

	PRIMARY WINNERS	NOMINEES	PRESIDENT
1952:	R – EISENHOWER D – KEFAUVER	EISENHOWER STEVENSON	EISENHOWER
1956:	R – EISENHOWER D – KEFAUVER	EISENHOWER STEVENSON	EISENHOWER
1960:	D – KENNEDY R – NIXON	KENNEDY NIXON	KENNEDY
1964:	D – JOHNSON* R – LODGE*	JOHNSON GOLDWATER	JOHNSON
1968:	R – NIXON D – JOHNSON*	NIXON HUMPHREY	NIXON
1972:	R – NIXON D – MUSKIE	NIXON McGOVERN	NIXON
1976:	D – CARTER R – FORD	CARTER FORD	CARTER
1980:	R – REAGAN D – CARTER	REAGAN CARTER	REAGAN
1984:	R – REAGAN D – HART	REAGAN MONDALE	REAGAN
1988:	R – BUSH D – DUKAKIS	BUSH DUKAKIS	BUSH
1992:	D – TSONGAS R – BUSH	CLINTON BUSH	CLINTON
1996:	D – CLINTON R – BUCHANAN	CLINTON DOLE	CLINTON
2000:	R – McCAIN D – GORE	BUSH GORE	BUSH

*Write-in.

National Convention Delegates 1952–2000

	NH		U.S.	
	R	D	R	D
1952:	14	8	1206	1230
1956:	14	8	1323	1372
1960:	14	11	1331	1521
1964:	14	20	1308	2316
1968:	8	26	1333	2622
1972:	14	18	1348	3016
1976:	21	17	2259	3008
1980:	22	19	1994	3331
1984:	22	22	2235	3933
1988:	23	22	2277	4162
1992:	23	24	2210	4288
1996:	16	26	1990	4289
2000:	17	29	2066	4339

Source: *National Party Conventions 2000*. CQ Press, 2001. Washington, DC.

Presidential Primary Dates   Candidates on the Ballot

Presidential Primary Dates	R	D
March 11, 1952	4	2
March 13, 1956	1	1
March 8, 1960	1	2
March 10, 1964	5	0
March 12, 1968	9	4
March 7, 1972	4	5
February 24, 1976	2	7
February 26, 1980	7	5
February 28, 1984	5	22
February 16, 1988	12	25
February 18, 1992	25	36
February 20, 1996	22	21
February 1, 2000	14	16

Source: New Hampshire Department of State.

Primary Turnout

	Registered	Voters R	D	Total	% of Total
1952:	317,368	92,865	36,252	129,117	40.7
1956:	323,625	57,064	25,646	82,710	25.6
1960:	325,885	73,031	50,899	123,930	38.0
1964:	349,667	92,853	30,777	123,630	35.4
1968:	363,503	103,938	55,470	159,408	43.9
1972:	423,822	117,208	88,854	206,062	48.6
1976:	443,583	110,190	81,525	191,715	43.2
1980:	509,915	146,534	111,595	258,129	50.6
1984:	488,970	75,240	101,045	176,285	36.1
1988:	586,492	157,643	123,512	281,155	47.9
1992:	570,982	173,419	167,664	341,083	59.7
1996:	688,445	208,740	91,027	299,767	43.5
2000:	783,594	238,206	154,639	392,845	50.1

Source: New Hampshire Department of State.

Bibliography of the New Hampshire Presidential Primary.

Beagle, M. J. *The New Hampshire Primer.* Warner: Moose Country Press, 1995.

Brereton, Charles. *First Step to the White House: The New Hampshire Primary 1952–1980.* Hampton: Wheelabrator Foundation, 1979.

———. *First in the Nation: New Hampshire and the Premier Presidential Primary.* Portsmouth: Peter E. Randall Publisher, 1987.

———. *First Primary: Presidential Politics in New Hampshire.* Manchester: Union Leader Corp., 1987. Updated by Donn Tibbetts, 1995.

Casey, Susan. Hart and Soul: *Gary Hart's New Hampshire Odyssey . . . and Beyond.* Concord: NHI Press, 1986.

Churgin, Jonah. *From Truman to Johnson: New Hampshire's Impact on American Politics.* New York: Yeshiva University Press, 1972.

Duncan, Dayton. *Grass Roots: One Year in the Life of the New Hampshire Presidential Primary.* New York: Viking, 1991.

Gregg, Hugh. *The Candidates: See How They Run.* Portsmouth: Peter E. Randall Publisher, 1990.

———. *A Tall State Revisited: A Republican Perspective.* Nashua: Resources of New Hampshire, Inc., 1993.

Hoeh, David. *1968 • McCarthy • New Hampshire: I Hear America Singing.* Rochester, MN: Lone Oak Press, Ltd., 1994.

LeBoutillier, John and Humes, James. *Primary.* New York: Manor Books, 1979.

Library & Archives of New Hampshire's Political Tradition. *New Hampshire's Political Troubadour.* Nashua: Resources of New Hampshire, Inc., 1999.

Orren, Gary and Polsby, Nelson, editors. *Media and Momentum:*

The New Hampshire Primary and Nomination Politics. Chatham, NJ: Chatham House Publishers, Inc., 1987.

Palmer, Niall. *The New Hampshire Primary and the American Electoral Process.* Boulder, CO: Westview Press, 1997.

Sherman, Steve. *Primary Crime.* Hancock: Appledore Books, 2000.

Wetherell, W.D. *The Wisest Man in America.* Hanover: University Press of New England, 1995.

ACKNOWLEDGMENTS

This is my fourth book on the New Hampshire first-in-the-nation presidential primary. Having been a resident of this state for 34 years, I am blessed with some wonderful friendships, most formed not long after moving here in 1969 from California.

Among those friends are Lafayette and Mayme Noda of Meriden, David and Heather Bower of Nelson, William and Fran D'Alessandro of Amherst, Richard and Pam Hunsberger of Pittsfield, Marian Woodruff of Randolph, Kathy Connor of Manchester and Peter Powell of Lancaster.

In my hometown of Concord over the years I have collaborated with John Gfroerer on a number of documentary projects. I have found each project to be a challenge and I am grateful for the opportunity to work with him as well as with his partner, Lisa Brown.

I would also like to thank several other individuals residing in this city: John Hoar, Victoria Zachos and Will and Natale Brown.

David Hoeh, author of *1968 • McCarthy • New Hampshire* has reassembled his family in the quaint village of Belmont, Vermont, in the central part of the Green Mountain State. There are a lot of special places to live and visit in northern New England and Belmont is one of them—almost as nice a place to stay as Eastport, Maine. David has my gratitude as well.

Thanks also to all those who agreed to be interviewed.

As with my previous books, the staffs of both the New Hampshire State Library and the Concord Public Library have been of great help, particularly those who have answered so many questions from the reference desks in both institutions.

Although she has departed from her post as the assistant director of the Library and Archives of New Hampshire's Political

Tradition, Trina Purcell has been a great help. The individuals responsible more than any others for the establishment of this group (www.PoliticalLibrary.org), former governor Hugh Gregg and the New Hampshire secretary of state, William Gardner, deserve the thanks of all citizens of this state for the founding of this much-needed organization to both preserve and celebrate the heritage of the primary.

I would like to acknowledge the assistance of Anne Nute for her ability to improve on the manuscript that has been presented to her.

Peter E. Randall Publisher of Portsmouth has published two previous works of mine. Randall now has more than 400 books under his imprint, the first one in 1970. All the citizens of this state are blessed by the literary legacy Peter has established on its history, culture and people.

Finally, in attending hundreds of campaign events on the primary trail since 1971, I have yet to attend an event where the individuals have not conducted themselves with grace and dignity. I doubt the same statement could be made if I'd lived in any other state instead, which is a remarkable testimony about the people who reside in what was one of the 13 original colonies. On June 21, 1788, the Granite State became the ninth and therefore deciding state to ratify our federal constitution. Therefore there is a long tradition of this small state's playing a significant role in determining how Americans govern themselves.

May it always be so.

Charles Brereton
Concord, New Hampshire
April 21, 2003

INDEX

About the Author

Charles Brereton is a writer living in Concord, New Hampshire, where he has resided since 1970, shortly after moving to the Granite State from California.

Mr. Brereton is the author of the book *First in the Nation: New Hampshire and the Premier Presidential Primary*, published in 1987 by Peter E. Randall of Portsmouth, New Hampshire. This 277-page book is one of the most extensive accounts of the primary, which has often had a significant impact on the course of American presidential politics.

Another of Brereton's books is *New Hampshire Notables*, published in 1986 for the New Hampshire Historical Society by Peter E. Randall. This book features biographical sketches of 422 prominent citizens of the Granite State and is the fourth in a series that began in 1919 with subsequent editions in 1932 and 1955.

Mr. Brereton was also a researcher for the television program "The Premier Primary: New Hampshire and Presidential Elections 1952–1984," which first aired in 1987. This program has been updated with the four primaries from 1988 to 2000 and was completed in fall 2002.

In addition he was a researcher for the program "Sherman Adams: Yankee Governor," on the life of the late governor (1949–1953) of New Hampshire who also served as assistant to President Dwight Eisenhower from 1953 to 1958. This program first aired on May 11, 1990.

Brereton also worked as a researcher for the program "Powerful as Truth," on the life of William Loeb, controversial publisher of the *Manchester Union Leader*.

In 1999 Brereton helped research the program "Eastport:

Where America Begins Its Day," on this nation's easternmost city, a community in Washington County, Maine, on the border with New Brunswick, Canada. He has traveled extensively in northern New England as well as in the Canadian Maritimes.

Between the years 1994 and 2000 Brereton published a series of calendars of Ebbets Field, home of the Brooklyn Dodgers from 1913 to 1957. In 2001 he published a calendar called Real Diamonds, which featured a collection of 15 black-and-white photographs of 14 ballparks.

The author was born in New Haven, Connecticut, on December 14, 1947. A 1966 graduate of San Marcos High School in Santa Barbara, California, he attended Santa Barbara City College from 1966 to 1968. He has been a resident of New Hampshire since 1969 after briefly residing in Arizona and Connecticut.

He may be contacted at P.O. Box 307, Concord, NH 03302.